Craig Brown, co-author of the bestselling *The Book of Royal Lists*, also available from Sphere, is a freelance journalist whose work has appeared in *The Times Literary Supplement* and *The Times Educational Supplement*, *Homes and Gardens*, the *Observer*, *Tatler* and many other newspapers and magazines. David Brown, his brother, is an enthusiastic sportsman who used to play football, rugger, tennis and cricket at a competitive level. Now, at the age of twenty-two, he has retired from virtually all sporting activity, though he still enjoys going to race meetings and watching cricket.

*Also by Craig Brown (and Lesley Cunliffe) in Sphere Books:*

THE BOOK OF ROYAL LISTS

# The Book of Sports Lists

**CRAIG and DAVID BROWN**

SPHERE BOOKS LIMITED
London and Sydney

First published in Great Britain by
Arthur Barker Ltd 1983
Copyright © 1983 by Craig and David Brown
Published by Sphere Books Ltd 1984
30–32 Gray's Inn Road, London WC1X 8JL

TRADE
MARK

Printed and bound in Great Britain by
Cox & Wyman Ltd, Reading

# CONTENTS

# Contents

# Contents

# CONTENTS

# Contents

# CONTENTS

# CONTENTS

# ACKNOWLEDGEMENTS

For their help and encouragement, we would like to thank James Brown, Dan Maskell, Mary Peters, Jim Laker, Henry Cooper, Mark Thatcher, Frank Carson, Ian Wooldridge, Brian Johnston, Josh Gifford, Clare Francis, Joe Bugner, Barry Fantoni, Euan and Su Bowater, Julian Symons, Derek Dougan, Deborah Rogers, Mr Kelly and all the staff at the *Daily Mail* reference library, Madame Tussaud's, John Poland and Co Ltd, our editors Stephen du Sautoy and Steve Dobell, and all those who told us sporting stories.

*For our mother and father*

# A

*5 Odd Reasons for Games being **Abandoned***

### 1 A LOST BALL
In November 1980, a rugger match between Fiji and Tacuman had
to be abandoned when Senegakali, the Fijian fly-half, kicked the ball
so far out of the ground that it could not be found. A second ball was
not considered up to standard, and there was no such thing as a third
ball.

### 2 A SINKING
In 1912, both the Oxford and the Cambridge boats sank and the Boat
Race was abandoned.

### 3 AN AWKWARD ANNIVERSARY
The planned English football tour of South America, scheduled for
the summer of 1983, was called off at the end of the previous December. The proposed date for the match against Argentina had been 14
June – the first anniversary of the Argentinian surrender in the Falk-
lands.

### 4 AN ABSENCE OF ACTION
When Jim Mace met Joe Coburn in a bare-fist fight in Canada in the
late nineteenth century, both boxers resolutely refused to start the
attack. Instead, they stood for one hour and seventeen minutes oppo-
site one another, and then the fight was called off.

### 5 A WAR
On 4 August 1914, competitors in the Second International Six Day
Motorbike Trial were informed by telegram that the event was postponed indefinitely due to the outbreak of war. Most of the Press,
officials and riders had already arrived in Grenoble, France, where it
was to be held. All of them got back safely, though some of the bikes
were lost in the rush. The Second International did not then take
place until 1920.

ACTED

## 7 Sportsmen who have **Acted** Professionally

### 1 ARNOLD PALMER
Arnold Palmer appeared with Bob Hope in *Call Me Bwana*.

### 2 SHARON DAVIES
Sharon Davies played the part of a windsurfer in a silent comedy called *The Optimist* filmed in Mexico.

### 3 HENRY COOPER
Henry Cooper played the part of Mr John Gully, English pugilist, racehorse owner and MP in *Royal Flash*. He was required to have a fist fight with Oliver Reed, who played Bismarck.

### 4 JOHNNY WEISSMULLER
Johnny Weissmuller, who won Gold Medals in the 1924 and 1928 Olympics for the 100 metres and 400 metres freestyle, went on to become more famous as Hollywood's Tarzan.

### 5 GUILLERMO VILAS
Guillermo Vilas acted a tennis player in the film *Players*. This is the only time he has been seen to win Wimbledon.

### 6 JACK JOHNSON
Jack Johnson, the first black heavyweight boxing World Champion, went on to play the part of Othello on stage.

### 7 GRAHAM HILL
Graham Hill played the part of a helicopter pilot in the Alistair Maclean film, *Caravan to Vaccares*.

## 5 of the Silliest **Advertisements** Involving Sportsmen

### 1 BILLIE JEAN KING ADVERTISING TOOTHPASTE
The slogan was: 'If Colgate is just a kid's cavity fighter, how come Billie Jean King won't brush with anything else?'

## 2 WILT CHAMBERLAIN ADVERTISING NASAL SPRAY

Under a two-page picture of Wilt Chamberlain, the 7 ft 2 ins basketball star, was the slogan: 'There's only one Wilt the Stilt. Long Duration of Action and Virtually No Rebound Problems. And there's only one Aria nasal spray. Long Duration of Action with Virtually No Rebound Problems.'

## 3 BILL BEACH ADVERTISING PILLS

In 1886, advertisements in Australian magazines showed pictures of the champion sculler Bill Beach with his walrus moustache, with a caption underneath saying: 'THE INVINCIBLE!'

> Gentlemen – Feeling unwell during my training for the second contest with Edward Hanlan of Toronto, for the championship of the world, my trainer purchased for me Warner's Safe Cure and Safe Pills, and I was agreeably astonished at the great benefit which followed their use.
> signed: William Beach.
> Champion Sculler of the World.

## 4 TOMMY DOCHERTY ADVERTISING RAZORS

Under a picture of Docherty stroking his chin was the caption: 'I can honestly say it's the closest shave I've ever had.'

## 5 HENRY COOPER ADVERTISING AFTER SHAVE

'Splash it on all over for the great smell of Brut.' Cooper later suggested why he had been chosen: 'The reason they chose me,' he said, 'is that no one can call me poofy.'

## 5 Occasions on which Sports *Advertising* has Come to a Sticky End

## 1 RAZORS ON THE CRICKET GROUND

In 1980, Gillette decided to back out of cricket sponsorship, complaining that the public was now associating the name Gillette more with cricket than with razors.

## 2 LINGERIE ON THE GOLF COURSE

During the 1979 Colgate European Women's Golf Championship at Sunningdale, leading women golfers were asked to remove slogans for

'Lily of France' lingerie from their sun visors. At first they refused, but then, under pressure from the BBC, they either removed them or stuck tape over them.

### 3 CIGARETTES ON THE TENNIS COURT

In 1972 at Wimbledon, Rosie Casals was warned that in future she must not wear a heavily patterned dress with the letters 'VS' embroidered up and down one side. 'VS' stood for 'Virginia Slims'. The umpire on the Centre Court had only noticed it as Miss Casals warmed up. 'I did not feel that was the correct time to ask her to change,' he reported later.

### 4 PICK-ME-UPS IN THE BOXING RING

In 1973, under pressure from the BBC, Italian boxer Franco Zurlo was forced to stick tape over slogans for an Italian hangover cure in the interval after the first round of the European bantamweight title.

### 5 CONTRACEPTIVES ON THE RACECOURSE

The firm of Durex had a particularly difficult time in their efforts to break into sports advertising. First they tried to enter the world of racing, but the jockey club refused to sanction the title 'Durex' as a suitable name for a horse. They twice managed to apply the name of their product to a Formula 5000 racing car, but then the BBC intervened and stopped it.

## 4 Pieces of **Advice** to Sportsmen

### 1 'Kick the other guy in the shins, belt him in the crotch if need be, but win.'

Big Daddy's father's advice to the young Big Daddy.

### 2 'Stay pretty. Whatever happens, stay pretty.'

Muhammad Ali's advice to Joe Bugner, before Bugner's fight with Winston Allen in October 1982.

### 3 'You should get high on life, not on drink.'

Paul McCartney's advice to John Conteh at a party in May 1981. Conteh had been talking about getting high on drink. Conteh had recently emerged from an alcoholism clinic. 'I intend to follow Paul's advice,' he said.

## 4 'Kill yourself.'

Skiing coach Tony Sailer's advice to Franz Klammer during the 1976 Winter Olympics. Klammer's fellow competitor Bernard Russie had just gone downhill in such a fast time that for a while it was assumed that the electronic timing device had fused. Klammer won.

### 6 of the Best Insults by *Muhammad Ali*

1 **'I've seen him shadow boxing and the shadow won.'**
(*On George Foreman*)

2 **'This is the bear hunting season! You big ugly bear! You're the Chump and I'm the Champ!'**
(*To Sonny Liston*)

3 **'You so ugly that when you cry the tears run down the back of your head.'**
(*To Sonny Liston*)

4 **'You so ugly you have to sneak up on the mirror so it won't run off the wall.'**
(*To Sonny Liston*)

5 **'He's a tramp, a bum and a cripple, not worth training for. I'll take him in five.'**
(*On Henry Cooper. He did*)

6 **'Joe who did you say? ... Oh, Frazier. Yeah, I remember him. He's the one who leads with his face all the time.'**

## 6 Poems by **Muhammad Ali**

1  'This is the legend of Cassius Clay
   The most beautiful fighter in the world today.
   He talks a great deal and brags indeed
   Of a muscular punch that's incredible in speed.
   This brash young boxer is something to see
   And the heavyweight championship is his destiny.
   He *is* the greatest!'

   (*1963, before fighting Sonny Liston*)

2  'I've been away for three and a half years taking a rest
   Now I'm back in the ring and I'm the best'

   (*On his 29th birthday*)

3  'I like your show and I like your style
   But your pay's so bad I won't be back for a while'

   (*To Michael Parkinson at the end of a programme*)

4  'This might shock and amaze ya,
   But I'm gonna re-tire Joe Frazier'

   (*January 1974*)

5  'From all over the world they send their best
   To battle Ali for the ultimate test.
   Now merry olde England is sending her hero
   Big Joe Bugner, whose chances are zero.
   Now Big Joe, he can swing, he can roll
   But with Muhammad Ali in there, the ring is just too small.
   Since when could a bug handle a bee,
   A bee that's as pretty and as quick as me.
   Bugs fly through the air with the greatest of ease.
   But this is one bug who will be on his knees...'

   (*1973*)

6  'We'd be better off if we obeyed God's command and
   Ate vegetables and grain and fruit of the land.

You may think fresh pork is a very rare treat
But our bodies are made of just what we eat.

And the food that the hog has eaten, which is the filth of the land,
Goes into our body as second hand.'

(*From a poem against pork*)


## 8 *Great* **All-Rounders**

1  CHARLES BURGESS FRY (1872–1956)
In 1893, Fry equalled the world record for the long jump. He represented England at soccer in 1901. He played first-class Rugby for the Barbarians. He captained the English cricket team in 1912, heading the batting averages for six seasons. He was later a delegate to the League of Nations and was once invited to be the King of Albania, an honour he refused.

2  JUDI DOULL
The New Zealand cricketer has also represented her country at hockey and at basketball.

3  EDDIE CHARLTON
Best known now as a snooker player, he was for ten years in first-grade soccer. In 1950 he was in the Australian surfing championship with the Swansea Belmont crew. He carried the Olympic torch in 1956. He was also successful in competitive cricket, athletics, tennis and speed rollerskating. He showed off his boxing prowess in a professional exhibition match with Dave Sands, the world middleweight champion.

4  J. P. R. WILLIAMS
The former Welsh full-back once won Junior Wimbledon when he was a schoolboy tennis player.

5  BOB SUTHERLAND
The winner of the 1983 Embassy World Indoor Bowls Crown was once the centre-half for Glasgow Rangers.

6 CHARLOTTE 'DOTTIE' DODD (1871–1960)
Charlotte 'Dottie' Dodd won the Wimbledon singles title five times.
She also won the British Ladies Golf Championship and an Olympic
Silver Medal for archery. In 1899 she represented England at hockey.

7 ANN JONES
The winner of Wimbledon in 1969 had previously been the top English
woman table-tennis player. She was a finalist in the 1957 World
Doubles and Singles Table-Tennis finals.

8 MILDRED DIDRIKSON
Mildred 'Babe' Didrikson is said to have broken the world record the
very first time she threw the javelin. In the 1932 Olympics she won
Gold Medals for the javelin and the 80 metres hurdles and a Silver
Medal for the high jump. She went on to become the leading female
golfer in America.

## 4 *Amateurs* who Became too Professional

1 KARL SHRANZ
In 1972, at the Winter Olympics in Sapporo, the Austrian skier Karl
Shranz was disqualified for permitting the use of his name and
photographs of himself in commercial advertising. When he arrived
back home in Vienna, a crowd of over 200,000 was there to greet him.

2 DWIGHT STONES
Tempted by a fee of $33,000 to appear on the television show *Superstars*
in 1977, the American high jumper plotted to circumvent any infringe-
ment to his amateur status by forming a charity called 'The Desert
Oasis Track Club'. The sole beneficiary of this charity was to be
Dwight Stones. But the American Amateur Athletics Union discovered his ploy and suspended him. Stones then threatened them
with court action. In reply, the Union said that if the money was to go
to a charity, then it should be them. Stones then withdrew his action
and was reinstated as an amateur athlete.

3 JIM THORPE
The American Football star Jim Thorpe was ordered to return his two

1912 Pentathlon and Decathlon Gold Medals after it was discovered that he had played two semi-professional baseball games. As a further rebuff, his name was removed from the records. Only thirty years after his death, in 1983, did the Amateur Athletics Union restore his amateur athletic status, which in turn allowed them to return his medals. But he was only restored to the official records as 'co-winner'.

4 LEE Q. CALHOUN
In 1958, Lee Q. Calhoun of the USA, the only man to win the Olympic 110 metres hurdles twice, was suspended by the Amateur Athletics Union for appearing with his bride on a television quiz show and receiving nearly £1,000 worth of free gifts.

### ... and innumerable Rugby Union Players
In September 1982, in Michael Alan Burton's autobiography *Never Say Die* came the revelation of undercover payments to amateur and professional sports stars. Adidas were prompted by this revelation to write to all their secret clients saying that they had forwarded details of the sums they had paid under the counter to the Inland Revenue. In Rugby Union, Burton alleged that £3,500 a boot was the going rate. He also alleged that Gareth Edwards had been the go-between for Adidas and the players.

## 5 Unusual **Ambitions** of Sportsmen

1 PLAYING THE PIANO
'I'd have given my right arm to have been a pianist,' Bobby Robson has admitted.

John Francome is still keen to get his piano playing good enough to be able to accompany his favourite singer, Miss Debbie Harry. It is perhaps more likely that he will accomplish his other ambition – to ride six winners in one afternoon's racing.

2 ROVING THE WORLD
On being defeated by Trevor Berbick in 1981, Muhammad Ali said that he would not be fighting again, but that his plans for the future included touring the world and 'speaking with people like Brezhnev – prestigious stuff.'

### 3 WALKING ON WATER
After he had won seven Olympic Gold Medals for swimming, Mark Spitz was asked if he'd ever thought of walking on water. 'If I could perfect it, it would really help my name,' he replied.

### 4 PLAYING FOR NOTTINGHAM FOREST
Derek Randall, who prefers football to cricket, has long held an ambition to play for Nottingham Forest.

### 5 SIRING A CHAMPION
Johnny Miller wants his son, John jr, to be the greatest golfer who ever lived. 'No famous golfer has had a son who made it,' he says. 'Mine will, even if I have to give up the game to help him.' John jr is twelve years old.

## 6 *Animals* which have Interfered with Sport

### 1 AN AFGHAN HOUND
In the summer of 1980, staying with her family in Spain, Sue Barker was mauled by an Afghan hound. The dog bit her twice, on the cheek and on the eye. For seven hours she lost the sight of her right eye and faced the possibility that her tennis career was over. She fully recovered after undergoing fifteen stitches.

### 2 A BIRD
In November 1969, John Inverarity, playing in an Australian interstate match, was clean bowled by a ball which had hit a bird flying over the pitch and had bounced on to the stumps. A benevolent umpire gave him 'Not Out'.

### 3 A COW
During a knock-up before a local cricket match at Pentenstall, Bedfordshire, in 1955, a player hit the cricket ball into a field, whereupon it was eaten by a cow called Bessie. The game had to be abandoned, as it was the club's only ball.

### 4 A TERRIER
In the middle of an FA Cup tie, a terrier rushed on to the pitch.

Liverpool manager Bob Paisley immediately got up and chased it around the pitch, but he admitted later that he had been using it as an excuse to talk to two or three of his players.

## 5 A PIG
During England's disastrous seven-wicket defeat against Australia in the fourth one-day international in January 1983 at Brisbane, a witty spectator let a small pig loose on the pitch. On one side of the pig's body was stamped 'Botham', and on the other, 'Eddie'. Both Ian Botham and Eddie Hemmings had been accused of being overweight.

## 6 A SMALL DOG
In a football match between Brentford and Colchester in 1970, a small dog ran on to the pitch and tackled Chris Brodie, damaging his cruciate ligaments and ending his career. 'If I ever catch up with that bloody animal,' said Brodie, 'I'll blow its backside off with a shotgun.'

## 4 Sporting **Apologies**

## 1 SORRY WE WERE VULGAR
After Brian Clough had criticized Nottingham Forest fans for singing dirty songs on the terraces, a group of them held up a banner saying simply, 'Sorry Brian'.

## 2 SORRY I WAS TASTELESS
At the Sports Writers Association dinner in 1976, John Curry walked in as comedian Roger de Courcey was making an after-dinner speech. 'There is no fairy at the top of the Christmas tree,' said de Courcey, 'but one has just walked in.' Curry then walked out. 'I am profoundly sorry,' said de Courcey later. He promised to send Curry a written apology.

## 3 SORRY ABOUT HIM
At the Sixth Test in Adelaide in 1972, when Geoff Boycott was given run out he threw his bat on the ground and stood with his hands on his hips. After the match, he refused to apologize, and tempers were only calmed when Ray Illingworth apologized on his behalf.

### 4 SORRY I WAS RUDE

In May 1973, playing an exhibition match in Sydney, Alex Higgins said of 63-year-old Norm Squires, whom he had beaten three times, 'He's an old no-hoper.' For this he was thrown out of the club. He was only allowed back after he had sat in a gutter and written an apology on a piece of toilet paper.

## 5 Sportsmen who have been **Assailed**

### 1 ERIC BRISTOW

When a man came up to Eric Bristow in a pub and said, 'You play darts, but can you fight?' Bristow replied, 'No, but I can afford to pay somebody to fight you for me.'

### 2 SUE BARKER

Sue Barker was once attacked by a mugger on a Detroit escalator, but she managed to fend him off with her tennis racket.

### 3 STEVE DAVIS

On 4 November 1981, Steve Davis had to flee a gang of skinheads as he signed autographs in Belfast. They also spat at him and kicked his car while he was driving off.

### 4 IAN BOTHAM

In September 1982, Ian Botham was thrown into a swimming pool at the Cadbury Country Club, Weston-super-Mare, by a 30-year-old motor mechanic, Mr Bent. Bent later told friends that he thought Botham was behaving arrogantly.

### 5 ILIE NASTASE

After the 1979 US Open Championships in September 1979, Vitas Gerulaitis, Ilie Nastase and Martina Navratilova went to Studio 54 in New York. While chatting with a blonde girl, Nastase was butted in the face by her boyfriend. Gerulaitis came in between the two to prevent a fight, and the blonde girl and her boyfriend were shown the door by owner Steve Rubell.

## 3 Sporting Comments on *Australians*

1 'They are Capital Winners out here: but I am afraid I cannot Apply the same Adjective to them as Losers.'
*Lord Harris, after a riot had followed the dismissal of an Australian batsman in 1879.*

2 'In my opinion Melburnians are like Piranha Fish when it comes to Sport. They will Devour Anything that will Satisfy their Appetite for Competition.'
*John Snow.*

3 'Australians can, and do, Quite Readily and Often in my Experience, throw off all their 180 years of Civilized Nationhood; they gaily revive every Prejudice they ever knew, Whether to do with Accent, Class Consciousness or even the original Convict Complex, and Sally Forth into Battle with a Dedication which would not Disgrace the most Committed of the World's Political Agitators.'
*Ted Dexter in Wisden, 1972.*

# B

## 6 Cases of Extreme *Bad Luck*

### 1 THE LONG-DISTANCE WALKER AND THE FREIGHT TRAIN

In the 1959 New Zealand Long Distance Walking Championships, Olympic Gold Medallist Norman Read was coming a close second to leader Kevin Keogh when a freight train passed between them. Read had to stand and wait while no fewer than 1,289 wagons chugged by.

### 2 THE BRUISED REFEREE AND THE SOCIAL SECURITY OFFICE

In 1978, wrestling referee John Ardron had a double dose of bad luck. First, Giant Haystacks threw him to the floor and then jumped on him after he had been disqualified. This caused bruising to Ardron's ribs. Second, an alert Social Security Officer, noticing a photograph of the bruised Ardron in the local newspaper, took him to court for failing to declare his income.

### 3 THE AUSTRALIAN JOCKEY AND THE MULTIPLE INJURIES

In twenty-seven years of racing, Australian jockey Fred Dummett fractured his right thigh in three places, broke his wrist, foot, leg and every one of his ribs, had his right cartilage removed and broke his collar-bone twenty-nine times.

### 4 THE GOLF SPECTATOR AND THE MAGNETIC GOLF BALLS

In 1962, Mr George Forest was hit twice while watching an exhibition match at Bathgate, West Lothian. At the second hole he was hit in the ribs by a shot from Charles Green. And then at the eleventh hole he was hit on the head by a drive from Gordon Cosh. After receiving stitches in hospital, Mr Forest, 64, commented, 'I've always been unlucky at that course. I've been struck five times in all.'

### 5 THE TENNIS PLAYER AND THE INEFFICIENT TRANSPORT

Trying to get from her London hotel to Wimbledon in 1982, tennis player Joanne Russell's taxi failed to turn up. Eventually, she managed to hitch a lift from a motorist. The car caught fire. She was then forced to lie down in the road to stop another car. An hour and forty minutes late, and terrified she would be disqualified, she ran into Wimbledon only to discover that her third-round match against Pam Casale had been postponed due to rain.

## 6  THE CRICKETER AND THE UNBENEFICIAL BENEFIT
At his benefit match against Somerset at Lord's in 1907, Albert Trott took two hat-tricks in the same innings, thus severely shortening the game and depriving himself of much gate money. 'I'm bowling myself into the workhouse,' he moaned.

## 7 *Bad Sports*

### 1  THE POLES
After Helen Stephens (USA) had won the Women's 100 Metre Dash at the Berlin Olympics in 1936, beating the Polish favourite Stella Walsh, the Poles started to accuse Miss Stephens of being a man in disguise. Eventually, she had to be examined in the nude. It was unanimously decided that she was a woman.

### 2  ROSIE CASALS
Playing Virginia Wade in Virginia, Rosie Casals became so bad-tempered that when they shook hands at the net at the end of the game she started to scream at her and refused to let go of her hand.

### 3  THE ARGENTINIANS
During the 552 matches in the 1980 Argentine Rugby Championship, no fewer than 251 players were sent off.

### 4  NORMAN HUNTER
Having kicked David Cross in the head in a Leeds v. Coventry match in 1975, Norman Hunter shouted, 'Just as well I hit you on the head, Crossie, or I might have hurt you.'

### 5  CLIFF THORBURN
During the 1981 World Snooker Championship semi-final, Cliff Thornburn said to Steve Davis, 'You have as much class as my backside.'

6  THE EL SALVADORIANS
El Salvador declared war on Honduras after the two sides had met in
a soccer match in 1969.

7  JAN STEPHENSON
Once, when Jan Stephenson missed a short putt, she kicked a rubbish
bin so hard that her foot went right through it and stuck there.

## 7 *Stages in the Romance between* **Sue Barker** *and* **Cliff Richard**

1  Early in 1982, The Reverend Alan Godson advises Sue to talk with
Cliff about her faith.
2  In April, Cliff says that he 'might be in love' with Sue and that
marriage is 'always possible'.
3  The Reverend Alan Godson says, 'It's the Good News story to end
them all, isn't it? I'm very happy for them both. It's a romance that
has a beauty all of its own.'
4  In June, Cliff says, 'Someone has to take over from Charles and Di.'
5  In August, Sue says, 'I'm not saying whether I'm in love with Cliff
or not . . . but our relationship is in its infancy.'
6  On 25 August, Cliff says, 'We are definitely not getting married yet.
I have never talked about marriage to her. I don't know her feelings
yet.'
7  On 28 August, Sue says, 'I'm never going to marry him. I never
even considered it.'

## 9 *Jobs of* **Jonah Barrington** *before he took up Squash*

1  Teacher in Spain.
2  Groundsman.
3  Coalman in Cornwall.
4  Cottage painter in Devon.
5  Carpet cleaner in London.
6  Schoolmaster in York.

7 Milkman in Earls Court.
8 Dishwasher.
9 Nude model.

## 11 Strange Reasons why Sportsmen have been **Barred**

### 1 A Sex Change
When Richard Raskind changed his sex to become Renee Richards in 1977, she was barred from entering the US Open Tennis Championships. After Miss Richards took her case to court, the judge ruled in her favour, calling the organizers 'grossly unfair, discriminative and inequitable'.

### 2 Being Lower Class
J.B. Kelly, the father of Princess Grace, was barred from the Henley Regatta of 1920, as Henley's patron, Prince Albert, had originally decreed that anyone who was 'by trade or employment for wages, a mechanic, artisan or labourer' was ineligible. Kelly won the Olympic Gold Medal in the same year, and in a fit of fury posted his sweaty cap to King George V.

### 3 Being Black
In 1912, Jack Johnson, the first black World Heavyweight Champion, was refused permission to board the *Titanic* because of his colour.

### 4 Poverty
As a child, Billie Jean King was so poor that the first time she was going to be in a tennis group photograph she was refused permission to pose, as she only had a blouse and a pair of shorts made by her mother, and not the obligatory whites.

### 5 Bragging
In January 1979, ex-welterweight boxer Bernie Simmonds barred Peter Osgood from his pub, 'The Wolf', in Windsor. 'I'm sick and tired of the name Osgood,' said Simmonds. 'He is always shooting his mouth off. If I continue to let him in I shall lose good customers.'

## 6 RELIGION, SEX AND POLITICS
Bullfighter Henry Higgins' book *To Be a Matador* was banned in Spain on religious, sexual and political grounds.

## 7 LETTING GIRLS IN
In August 1982, Malcolm Allison was suspended by his club, Sporting Lisbon, for allegedly allowing girls into the team's quarters on their tour of Bulgaria. 'The stories are complete fabrication,' he complained. 'Yet the rumours and innuendoes have multiplied.'

## 8 UNSEEMLY BEHAVIOUR
In 1981, John McEnroe was denied membership of the All England Lawn Tennis Club because of his unseemly behaviour.

## 9 TOO MUCH FAME
Triple Grand National winner Red Rum was barred from making a guest appearance at the 1980 Grand National. The organizers feared that he would steal the limelight from the other runners.

## 10 ATTACKING OFFICIALS
In May 1979, Alan Evans was banned from all darts contests for a year by the Welsh Darts Organization for attacking an official in the Wales v. England match at Pembroke. 'I'm disillusioned,' he said.

In 1972, Jeff Thomson was banned worldwide from all football. While captaining a church football team, he settled an argument with a referee by breaking his nose. The ban has since been lifted.

## 11 DRUNKENNESS
In 1897, the captain of Yorkshire Cricket Club, Lord Hawke, imposed a ban on left-arm spinner Bobby Peel as a punishment for his drunkenness. Peel had come on to the pitch and urinated in front of the captain.

# BBC

### The **BBC** Sports Personalities of the Year
*(The award was inaugurated in 1954. It is voted for by an average of 100,000 'Radio Times' readers each December.)*

| | | | |
|---|---|---|---|
| 1954 | Christopher Chataway | 1969 | Ann Jones |
| 1955 | Gordon Pirie | 1970 | Henry Cooper |
| 1956 | Jim Laker | 1971 | Princess Anne |
| 1957 | Dai Rees | 1972 | Mary Peters |
| 1958 | Ian Black | 1973 | Jackie Stewart |
| 1959 | John Surtees | 1974 | Brendan Foster |
| 1960 | David Broome | 1975 | David Steele |
| 1961 | Stirling Moss | 1976 | John Curry |
| 1962 | Anita Lonsborough | 1977 | Virginia Wade |
| 1963 | Dorothy Hyman | 1978 | Steve Ovett |
| 1964 | Mary Rand | 1979 | Sebastian Coe |
| 1965 | Tommy Simpson | 1980 | Robin Cousins |
| 1966 | Bobby Moore | 1981 | Ian Botham |
| 1967 | Henry Cooper | 1982 | Daley Thompson |
| 1968 | David Hemery | | |

### **George Best's** Views on 6 of the Women in his Life

1 EVA HARALDSTED
'You could say I fell in love with a pair of knockers.'

2 MARJORIE WALLACE
'Not exactly a meeting of minds.'

'I wanted her because she was Miss World and she wanted me because I was George Best.'

3 SINEAD CUSACK
'One of the few I really liked.'

4 CAROLYN MOORE
'She was special.'

5 ANGIE BEST
'She's the first emotionally strong woman I've ever known ... yet she taught me how to cry.'

6 MARY STAVIN
'I think the world of her.'

## 6 Views on **George Best**

'**Once you get the taste of George Best you never want to taste another thing.**'
*Angie Best, September 1979.*

'**When he's boozing he's the most deplorable, obnoxious, sarcastic, ignorant, horrible piece of rubbish.**'
*Angie Best, February 1982.*

'**Let's get the record straight. I've never seen George the worse for drink. He doesn't smoke and he does train hard.**'
*Bobby Charlton, 1970.*

'**The trouble with George is he thinks he can fascinate any girl who comes within a mile of him.**'
*Stefanja Sloniecka, January 1973.*

'**Really he's still the same little boy lost that he was when he first came to Manchester.**'
*Mrs Fullaway, Best's former landlady in Manchester, August 1982.*

'**He's one of the most intelligent, considerate and generous of men. I still love him, but there are problems better solved on his own.**'
*Mary Stavin, on leaving Best, May 1983.*

## 6 Sportsmen who have **Bet** on Themselves

1 STAN BOWLES
At the start of the 1975-76 season, Stan Bowles backed his club, Queen's Park Rangers, to win the championship. He bet £6000 at 16-1. They didn't win.

2 WILLIAM GILBERT
William Gilbert placed all his money on his horse Sailor Prince to win the Royal Hunt Cup at Ascot. It had already won the 2,000 Guineas. But Sailor Prince lost. The winner was another horse owned by Gilbert. Its name was Despair.

3 CLIFF THORBURN
In 1977, Cliff Thorburn backed himself at 18-1 for £350 to win the Embassy World Professional Snooker Championship. He lost to John Spencer.

4 JACK DEMPSEY
Fighting the World Heavyweight title in 1919, Jack Dempsey bet his whole purse at 10-1 that he would knock out Jess Willard in the first round. Willard stayed on until the third round.

5/6 STAN BOWLES AND MALCOLM MACDONALD
In 1976, Stan Bowles of Queen's Park Rangers and Malcolm Macdonald of Arsenal had a £500 bet on who would get most goals in that season. Macdonald won.

### ... and Three Sportsmen who Bet on their Opponents

When England looked in dire straits during the third Cornhill Test in 1981, Australians Dennis Lillee and Rodney Marsh backed England to win at 500-1. When England won, and news of their bet leaked out, there was considerable outcry.

Worcestershire County Cricket Club dismissed former Pakistan Test player Younis Ahmed for gross misconduct following allegations that he placed a £100 bet on Worcester to lose a John Player League match at Leicester on 8 May 1983.

## 8 *Bizarre* Sports which are Regularly Played

### 1 THE WORLD HAGGIS HURLING CHAMPIONSHIP
Each October, the World Haggis Hurling Championship is organized by the World Haggis Hurling Association. The haggises must all weigh one and a half pounds and be deep frozen. In 1980, an official measuring the length of a hurl was knocked out when another haggis hit him.

### 2 CHRISTMAS DAY CRICKET
Every Christmas Day for the last forty-five years two teams – The Yule Logs and the Noel Bennet XI – have played cricket at Brighton.

### 3 INDIAN KICKBALL
Indian kickball is regularly contested between the Mexicans and the Hopis. The course is up to forty miles and each team has to kick a ball the whole length.

### 4 THE ANNUAL TODD RIVER REGATTA
The Annual Regatta on Todd River, Alice Springs, is generally held in the absence of any water. The competitors simply pick up their boats and run. During a drought, the yachting section consists of sailors stepping into bottomless boats, gripping the sides and running.

### 5 BLIND GOLF
In December 1982, the Royal National Institute for the Blind formed an Association of Blind Golfers. The twenty-five members play with sighted golfers who tell them the directions and distances. At the putting stage, a sonic bleeper is placed near the hole.

### 6 BUZKASHI
In the Afghan handball game of buzkashi the ball is made of the skin of a ritually slaughtered goat, filled with sand. The game is played on horseback. The riders may whip each other but not each other's horses.

### 7 NATIONAL RATTLE-SNAKE SACKING CONTEST
In the Annual National Rattle-snake Sacking Contest in America, the first prize goes to whoever manages to get ten rattle-snakes out of a central pit and into a sack without flinching or falling.

## 8 Bungy Jumping
'Bungy jumping' is the invention and regular pursuit of The Oxford Dangerous Sports Club. Participants attach bungy cord to their bodies and jump from vast heights. The Clifton Suspension Bridge, the Golden Gate Bridge and the Royal Gorge Bridge have all been leapt from on different occasions. 'I'm doing it because of the Boomtown Rats,' explained Lady Sophia Murphy before hurling herself off the Royal Gorge Bridge in March 1980. 'They made me realize that you have to experience everything in life.'

## 6 Sportsmen who have Enjoyed **Blowing their own Trumpets**

### 1 Freddie Trueman
When Freddie Trueman was asked to suggest a title for his autobiography, he replied: 'The Definitive Volume on the Finest Bloody Fast Bowler that Ever Drew Breath'.

### 2 Ray Reardon
Ray Reardon's car number plate is 1 PRO.

### 3 Marvin Hagler
In spring 1982, Marvin Hagler changed his name by deed poll from Marvin Nathaniel Hagler to Marvellous Marvin Hagler.

### 4 Martina Navratilova
In June 1982, Martina Navratilova claimed, 'I am the only woman who does not have a sweat problem.'

### 5 Muhammad Ali
Having won the Gold Medal for light-heavyweight boxing at the Rome Olympics, Ali returned to his home town of Louisville and said to the welcoming crowds, 'Look at me, am I not beauty? Inhale me, am I not perfume?'

### 6 Gold Belt Maxime
In 1970, Gold Belt Maxime said, 'A lot of wrestlers think they're God's gift to women. I'm different. I *know* I am.'

## 10 Memorable **Blunders** by Sports Commentators

1 'It's a desperately close race – I can't quite tell who is ahead
– it's either Oxford or Cambridge.'
*John Snagge, during the 1952 Boat Race.*

2 'The obvious successor to Brearley at the moment isn't
obvious.'
*Trevor Bailey.*

3 'The bowler's Holding, the batsman's Willey.'
*Brian Johnston on a Test match against the West Indies (Peter Willey was
facing Michael Holding).*

4 'I make no apologies for their absence but I'm sorry they're
not here.'
*Murray Walker.*

5 'Boycott, somewhat a creature of habit, likes exactly the
sort of food he himself prefers.'
*Don Mosey.*

6 'Michelle Ford ... is Australia's first Olympic medal for
four years.'
*Norman May.*

7 'She's dragged the javelin back into the twentieth century.'
*Ron Pickering.*

8 'The latest news here is that Warr's declared.'
*Brian Johnston, commentating on a Middlesex v. Sussex match.*

9 'You can cut that tension with a cricket stump.'
*Murray Walker.*

10 'If you hadn't been there it wouldn't have been much of a
fight.'
*Harry Carpenter to Ken Norton after he had lost to Ali in 1976.*

(Compiled with the help of Barry Fantoni, author of *Colemanballs*)

*The Years in which the Oxford or Cambridge Boats have Sunk during the **Boat Race***

1857  Cambridge

1912  Oxford and Cambridge

1925  Oxford

1951  Oxford

1978  Cambridge

*7 Facts in Favour of the 1932 **'Bodyline'** English Cricket Side*

1  HISTORY
Ten years before the 1932 tour, an English batsman had lost his wicket by being struck on the head by Gregory, the Australian fast bowler. But no one criticized the bowling then.

2  CAMPING IT UP
The Australian batsmen dramatized things, ducking at balls which were barely higher than the stumps.

3  THE ACCUSATION
Australians termed it 'bodyline' bowling. But all bowling is in some way aimed at the body.

4  INDIRECTNESS
The Australian Board of Control refused to discuss the issue with Jardine or Warner, complaining instead by cable to the MCC.

5  SOLIDARITY OF ENGLISH
All the English players stayed loyal to their captain.

## 6 DISUNITY OF AUSTRALIANS
One Australian batsman, S.J. McCabe, disassociated himself from the attacks, having found the proper batting defence. Others also disassociated themselves, including the great Australian wicket-keeper W.A. Oldfield.

## 7 OLD DOGS
The only English cricketers who complained were all in middle age, and consequently unable or unwilling to learn new tricks.

## The 10 Silliest Titles for Sports **Books**

1 *Pat on the Back*, by Pat Eddery
2 *Jack on my Back*, by Andrea Angela, Jack Nicklaus's former caddie
3 *Gosh it's Tosh*, an anthology of poems by John Toshack
4 *It's All about a Ball*, by Alan Ball
5 *Sods I have Cut on the Turf*, by Jack Leach
6 *Nice One Cyril*, by Cyril Knowles
7 *V is for Victory*, by Harvey Smith
8 *The Game with the Hole in It*, by Peter Dobereiner
9 *Football Makes me Laugh*, by Malcolm Macdonald
10 *Frame and Fortune*, by Steve Davis

## 10 Items Endorsed by **Bjorn Borg**

1 A Bjorn Borg doll (*USA*)
2 Saab cars (*worldwide*)
3 Sunkist soft drink (*Japan*)
4 Jockey clothes (*Scandinavia*)
5 Notebook pencil and rubber (*Scandinavia*)
6 Kellogs cereal (*Europe*)
7 Viking sewing machine (*worldwide*)

8  Bjorn Borg toy (*Brazil*)
9  Scandinavia Airlines (*Worldwide*)
10 Penn tennis balls (*Europe and South America*)

## *Bjorn Borg's* 5 *Superstitions*

### 1 THE BEARD
Four days before a championship he would stop shaving.

### 2 THE BAG
Before each match, he would pack his tennis bag with extraordinary exactitude. All ten racquets had to be piled in descending order of tension. This would usually take an hour of testing.

### 3 THE CAR
He would always travel to Wimbledon in a car with a stereo radio.

### 4 THE ROUTE
He would always go the same route to Wimbledon, always over Hammersmith Bridge, never Putney Bridge.

### 5 THE BOILED SWEET
His mother, Margarethe Borg, always sucked a boiled sweet while watching his final set. In 1979, after Borg had rallied to triple match point and Tanner had rallied to deuce, Margarethe spat her sweet on the floor. She then intuitively picked it up and put it in her mouth again. Sure enough, Borg won.

## 4 *Places that have Witnessed* **Bribery** *and Corruption*

### 1 MELBOURNE
It is more than likely that as many as fifteen out of the twenty cyclists in the Australian Wheel Race of 1901 had been bribed to lose. The man who organized the bribery, William Martin, known as 'The Plugger', won the race by a clear fifteen yards. Martin's trainer,

known as 'General Gordon', later described laying out piles of notes in a hotel room. Each cyclist was invited alone into the room to be faced by the notes and a revolver held by Martin. Before they took the money, they were required to sign a receipt.

## 2 BLANKENBERGHE

Before the First World War, Horatio Bottomley bought all six horses which had been entered in a race at Blankenberghe in Belgium. He then hired six English jockeys and gave them strict instructions as to the order in which they should cross the finishing line. As a final precaution, he backed all six horses. Alas, halfway through the race a thick sea mist blew inshore and blotted out the whole course. Neither jockeys nor judges could see a thing and the race was abandoned. Bottomley lost a fortune.

## 3 WOOLLAHRA

In 1973, the *Sydney Herald* reported that a leading Roman Catholic school had withdrawn its under-six team from the Junior Rugby League because of bribes by parents. The school was the Holy Cross Primary School in Woollahra, a wealthy eastern suburb. The school principal, Sister Mary Julian, told parents in a statement, 'A dollar for a tackle or a try, and more after the game, is common. It is a sick atmosphere and not one to be encouraged.'

The *Herald*'s headline ran: 'Rugby Tots Bribed Says Nun'.

## 4 EVERYWHERE BUT SPURS

At a Press conference in 1975, Bill Nicholson, the General Manager of Tottenham Hotspurs, alleged that players wouldn't go to his club because he always refused to give under-the-counter money. 'It is expected in the London area for players to ask for £7,000 tax free. That's the minimum,' he explained.

***James Brown's*** *List of the 10 Most Ingenious Names for Racehorses*

1 SWING THE AXE
*by No Mercy out of Beech Tree*

2 DRESSED TO KILL
*Sharpen Up – Boudoir*

3  ZEBRA CROSSING
*Pal's Passage – Jungle Law*

4  COLD BLOOD
*Great Nephew – Ice Ballet*

5  BLUE PATROL
*Queen's Hussar – Silk Stocking*

6  GYPSY INN
*Romany Air – Courage*

7  TEMPTING FATE
*Welsh Saint – Rollicking Rachel*

8  EJECTOR SEAT
*Space King – Hasty Decision*

9  DISCO BEAT
*No Mercy – Evening Shoe*

10  CHASTITY BELT
*So Blessed – Queen's Keys*

(James Brown, brother of the authors, has been a racing enthusiast since the age of five.)


***Joe Bugner's*** *10 Favourite Actors and Actresses and his Choice of their Best Films*

1  SEAN CONNERY (*The Man Who Would Be King*)
2  RICHARD HARRIS (*Camelot*)
3  ROBERT DE NIRO (*Raging Bull, The Godfather*)
4  ROBERT DUVALL (*The Godfather, parts 1 and 2*)
5  ROBERT SHAW (*The Deep*)
6  GEORGE C. SCOTT (*Islands in the Stream*)
7  LANA TURNER (*Portrait in Black*)
8  GLENDA JACKSON (*House Calls*)

9 VANESSA REDGRAVE (*Camelot, Julia*)
10 AVA GARDNER (*The Barefoot Contessa*)

Joe Bugner adds: 'These actors and actresses are not in order, but they are my favourites. I think they are very versatile and capable of handling any scripts put before them and making them sound and look as real as in a real-life situation.'

## 5 Films in which **Joe Bugner** has Starred

1 *Diamonds are as Red as Blood*
2 *Upper Cut*
3 *A Man Called Bulldozer*
4 *I am for the Hippopotamus*
5 *The Sherriff and the Satellite Kid*

## 5 **Business** Partnerships between Sportsmen

### 1 **Godfrey Evans and Jim Laker**
Partners in an insurance brokerage business.

### 2 **George Best and Mike Summerbee**
Partners in two boutiques specializing in Edwardian clothes.

### 3 **John Francome and Bill Shoemark**
Partners in 'The Covingham Fish Bar' in Covingham Square, Swindon.

### 4 **Geoff Hurst and Jimmy Greaves**
Partners in a football kit company.

### 5 **Bobby Moore and Sean Connery**
Partners in an Essex Country Club.

# C

*7 Odd **Calls** from Sports Crowds*

1 'Moo! Moo!'
The day after American golfer Dave Hill had criticized the US Open Course for 1970, at Chaska, by saying, 'All it needs is eighty acres of corn and some cows', he was greeted with shouts of 'Moo! Moo!' from local residents. He was later fined 150 dollars for his comments. As he was paying the fine he suggested that he should write a cheque for another 150 dollars – 'So that I can criticize it some more.'

2 'I hope you drive better than you speak!'
This was the response of a woman in the audience after Graham Hill had been speaking at the Guild of Professional Toastmasters Award Dinner, where he was collecting his award for the Best After Dinner Speaker of 1971.

3 'Peter Shilton, Peter Shilton, does your Missus know you're here?'
This was sung by Arsenal fans, to the tune of 'Bread of Heaven', after Peter Shilton had been discovered in a parked car with a married woman he had met in a nightclub in September 1980. As he was doing pre-match press-ups, the song was augmented with cries of 'Haven't you done enough press-ups?'

'Things happen in football and in life. You have to face them,' he philosophized.

4 'You lucky little South African!'
This was a call from the crowd in the Open Championship of 1981 to Gary Player. Player replied, 'You know, it's truly amazing. The more I practise, the luckier I get.'

5 'No rounders!'
Towards the end of the nineteenth century, Americans became so fed up with baseball being compared to girls' rounders by visiting English people, that in 1889 a meeting held to celebrate the return of a baseball

squad from a tour of England, Australia and Honolulu was addressed by a lecturer who declared that 'patriotism and research' had established that baseball was a game of American origin. The meeting ended with orchestrated audience cheering of 'No Rounders!'

6 'IF YOU GET US TO THE FINAL AGAIN NEXT YEAR, YOU CAN HAVE MY WIFE TOO!'
This was a call from a fan to Tommy Docherty in January 1982, shortly after the story of Docherty's affair with his team's physiotherapist's wife had made the headlines.

7 'USE BOTHAM TO ROLL THE PITCH!'
This was the message on a New Zealand banner in February 1983. It is believed to be a reference to Ian Botham's weight problem.

## *Frank Carson's* Top 5 Irish Sporting Jokes

1 Murphy done 100 meters in record time. He got six months. They were gas meters.
2 In the pole vault Cassidy done 18ft 5ins. He was disqualified. He didn't come down.
3 Did you hear about the Irish boxer who was so far behind on points he needed a knockout for a draw?
4 The river was so polluted the first fish O'Connor pulled out thanked him.
5 In the Irish Olympic Finals Flanagan took the first bend so fast his left wellie burst.

## 7 Sporting *Casanovas*

1 VIV RICHARDS
'In Britain I have a dozen or so girls who mean a good deal more to me than a one-night stand. I keep phone numbers religiously and when we're playing away I ring for a date. There are good friends in Nottingham, Cardiff, Birmingham, Manchester, London and, of course, Taunton.'

## 2 ERIC BRISTOW
'I'm young and healthy and free and you'd be amazed at the number of dishy birds at big darts events these days.'

## 3 TERRY BIDDLECOMBE
'I would be lying if I denied taking advantage of the pleasure offered to me. I indulged my rather passionate nature to the full, and loved every moment of it. Women have given me lots of enjoyment and laughter.'

## 4 ALEX HIGGINS
'I know I've got a reputation like George Best. I've found that it helps being world champion, especially at snooker. I always tell them I'm a great potter. They know what I mean.'

## 5 GEORGE BEST
Best once said that he had tried to count the girls he had slept with, but had lost count at five hundred. 'If you want the secret of my success with women,' he says, 'then don't smoke, don't take drugs and don't be too particular.'

## 6 GUILLERMO VILAS
'There are girls for one night, girls to live with, girls to take travelling. There are right girls for different moments. You can love a girl today, but maybe not tomorrow.'

## 7 SEVVY BALLESTEROS
'That would be like playing the same golf course all the time.' (On being asked why he didn't have just one girlfriend.)

## 2 Victory *Celebrations* which Proved Unnecessary

### 1 JOHN KELLY'S VICTORY CELEBRATION
In 1950, John Kelly, brother of Princess Grace and son of champion sculler J.B. Kelly, was so confident of winning the Philadelphia Challenge Cup that he organized a Victory Ball to take place the night before the race. During the ball, his father made a speech saying how

sorry he was for Mervyn Wood, a Sydney policeman who was the main challenger, but how he hoped that he would find that his trip had returned an investment, as a wise man always made capital of his failures.

Wood won the race easily.

## 2 THE BOSTON COLLEGE EAGLES' VICTORY CELEBRATION

On the morning of 28 November 1942, the Boston College Eagles football team reserved a room in the Coconut Grove night club for a victory celebration to take place after their match against The Holy Cross. But they were beaten 55–12. However, the following morning they were counting themselves lucky to have lost – hundreds of people had been killed when a fire broke out in the Coconut Grove. After losing, the Eagles had cancelled their booking.

# 13 *Cheats*

## 1 A RUSSIAN PENTATHLETE

At the 1976 Montreal Olympics, Boris Onishenko, the Russian pentathlete, was discovered to have rigged his épée with an electrical circuit to register non-existent hits. He was disqualified. He was then escorted back to the USSR by two KGB guards. He has not been heard of since, though some say that he is driving a taxi in Leningrad, while others maintain that he has committed suicide.

## 2 A GERMAN STUDENT

At the 1972 Munich Olympics, Norbert Sudhaus, a twenty-two-year-old German student, joined the marathon on the home stretch just outside the stadium and then ran past the finishing line to the cheers of the crowd. But his fraud was immediately discovered, and the man who had appeared to be coming a distant second, Frank Shorter, was declared the winner.

## 3 ALI'S MANAGER

When Henry Cooper knocked down Cassius Clay in 1963, he entered boxing history. Only recently, however, has Clay's manager Angelo Dundee added a footnote to that history. He has admitted that when Clay got up with a damaged glove he enlarged the damage to buy time while new gloves were found.

## 4 THREE EAST GERMAN TOBOGANNERS

At the 1968 Winter Olympics at Grenoble, three East Germans, including Ortrun Enderlein, the 1964 Women's Champion, were disqualified from the single-seater toboganning when it was discovered that they had heated the runners of their sleds over an open fire in an effort to attain greater speed.

## 5 AN AMERICAN RUNNER

At the 1904 Olympics in St Louis, USA, American marathon runner Fred Lorz got cramp after ten miles. He hitched a lift from a truck for the next nine miles and then continued running, trotting into the stadium well ahead of the rest of the field. He was about to be awarded the Gold Medal by Alice Roosevelt when the real winner, Tom Hicks, ran into the stadium and alerted officials to Lorz's knavery. Lorz said that he had meant to confess sooner but had been overcome by the adulation. He was banned from running for a year, but later went on to win the US Marathon Championship.

## 6 THE STUTTGART TWINS

Lookalike brothers Karl-Heinz and Bernd Forster were both suspended from football after Bernd had deceived a referee into thinking that he was Karl-Heinz. Karl-Heinz had already been cautioned once and a further booking would have entailed being sent off, so Bernd took his place. Their misdeed might not have been discovered had they not later boasted of it to reporters.

## 7 AN AMERICAN BASEBALL PLAYER

John McGraw of the notorious Baltimore Orioles used to hold on to his opponents' belts to stop their progress. But one day an opponent loosened his belt, leaving it dangling in McGraw's hand.

## 8 TWO GHANAIAN FOOTBALLERS

After a match against the Brazilian football club Palmeiras in July 1969, the Accra Great Olympic Football Club of Ghana admitted that they had had thirteen players on the field at one stage. 'An unfortunate accident,' said an official. 'The two extra players sneaked on to the field, pretending to replace injured colleagues.'

## 9 THE NEW YORK PUNTERS

In the 1920s, a barber shop at the Aqueduct Racecourse in New York State was closed down when it was discovered that punters were watching to see which trainers were going in for a shave in anticipation of a winner's photograph.

## 10 BOB PAISLEY

Bob Paisley has admitted that one of his tactics used to be to make signs from his dugout to particular players, telling them to go down with an injury after the next tackle. He would then run on to the pitch and hover round the referee, pointing out how many mistakes he had made, thus intimidating him towards favouring Liverpool.

## 11 TIGER LANCE

In a Johannesburg Test match, after Ian Chappell had been given out, caught by Tiger Lance, Chappell asked Lance if he had in fact caught the ball. Lance said that he had, and Chappell left the pitch. Drinking at the bar afterwards, Chappell approached Lance and once more asked him whether he had caught it. 'You never asked me whether the ball had bounced first,' replied Lance.

## 12 THE CHICAGO WHITE SOX

During the World Series in 1919, The Chicago White Sox baseball team, thinking their employer underpaid them, sought a gambler to pay them 10,000 dollars a man to lose their match against Cincinatti. They lost at 4-1 on. Later, eight players and Arnold Rothstein, self-styled 'King of Gamblers', were brought to trial. All of them were acquitted, though it was proved that Rothstein had won $350,000.

## 13 A BOGUS WOMAN

At the 1936 Olympics, after Dora Ratjen had won the women's high jump and had attained a new world record, it was discovered that she was in fact a man. Herman Ratjen, for it was he, claimed to have lived the life of a woman for three years, but this was seen as no excuse and his Gold Medal was withdrawn.

### 4 Sportsmen who were Helped by their **Clothes**

## 1 W. G. GRACE

At a match in Clifton, Bristol, in 1878, W.G. Grace ran with a cricket ball which had lodged in his shirt. He was stopped only after the fielders had pulled him to a halt. He excused himself by saying that if he had handled the ball he would have been given out.

## 2 A. R. GOVER

Jim Laker's first wicket in first-class cricket occurred when he was bowling against R.N. Exton at Kingston in 1946. Fielder A.R. Gover was putting a sweater over his head when the ball came his way. He caught it by closing his legs on it.

## 3/4 JEAN-PIERRE BLEINCHARD AND J. JEFFRIES

In January 1785, Jean-Pierre Bleinchard and J. Jeffries, making their first cross-channel balloon flight, were forced to remove some of their clothes and toss them overboard to avoid going down.

## *Brian Clough's* Views on his Football Associates

### 1 THE FOOTBALL ASSOCIATION
'When the FA get into their stride, they make the Mafia look like kindergarten material.'

### 2 THE BOARD
'There's a seven-man board at Derby and I wouldn't give you two-pence for five of them.'

### 3 THE PARTNER
'I am the shop front. He's the goods in the back.' (*On Peter Taylor*)

### 4 THE PLAYER
'Kenny Burns? He loves a little chuckle when I fine somebody else.'

## *Sebastian Coe's* Desert Island Discs

1 'History of a Boy Scout', by the Dave Brubeck Quartet
2 'A Sunday Afternoon at Home', by Tony Hancock

3 'Extract from *Tosca*, Act One', by Puccini
4 'Georgia on My Mind', by Billie Holiday
5 'Just a Closer Walk With Thee', by The Lawson-Haggart Greats of Jazz
6 'The 1980 Olympic Anthem'
7 'Love for Sale', by Sidney Bechet
8 'A Foggy Day in London Town', by Ella Fitzgerald, Louis Armstrong and Oscar Peterson

*Luxury*: A very, very comfortable bed
*Book*: *The Penguin Dorothy Parker*

## 7 Notable Sporting **Collapses**

### 1 DEVON LOCH
Up to 1956, no Royal horse had ever won the Grand National. In that year, Devon Loch, owned by the Queen Mother, was leading with only thirty yards to go. Suddenly his front legs leapt high in the air, possibly trying to jump an imaginary fence. He landed on his belly, and ESB overtook him and won. The jockey was Dick Francis.

### 2 THE AMERICAN SOCCER TRAINER
In the 1930 World Cup, the United States of America were beaten 6–1 by Argentina in the semi-final. The American trainer had become so infuriated by the play of Argentinian Luis Monti that he ran on to the pitch to remonstrate with the Belgian referee. In a fury, he threw his medicine chest to the ground and, so doing, smashed a bottle of chloroform. Overcome by the fumes, he subsided unconscious on to the pitch.

### 3 BOBBY GEORGE
In October 1981, Bobby George collapsed during a darts match and was rushed to an operating theatre. A doctor later told him that he had been five minutes from death: glandular fever had spread to his spleen.

'The bad joke is that it had to be me that was so ill,' George groused afterwards. 'I mean, just look at some of the other darts lads. They're a bit of a disgrace, aren't they, with the way they drink and smoke. Some of them will be lucky to see fifty.'

### 4 JIM PETERS

In the 1954 British Commonwealth Games in Vancouver, Jim Peters. the English marathon runner, was winning as he entered the stadium, but suddenly collapsed. His trainer ran up to him and took hold of him, an action for which Peters was disqualified.

### 5 JOHNNY MILLER

While playing the seventeenth hole at the Speedway Golf Course in Indiana in 1977, Johnny Miller collapsed. After he had been rushed to hospital, doctors said that the thirty-year-old Miller had had stomach spasms.

### 6 DORANDO PIETRI

In the 1908 London Olympics, Dorando Pietri entered the stadium at the end of the Marathon with only 385 yards to go, a full 600 yards ahead of his nearest rival. But as he entered he turned the wrong way. Officials blocked his passageway, setting him on the right course. After a few yards, he began to stagger all over the track, and then he fell. He got up, and fell again. This happened four times. Eventually he was helped to the finishing line by officials, and once he had crossed it he was put on a stretcher and taken to hospital. But he was disqualified, as the Marathon rules state that each runner must race unaided.

### 7 GIANT HAYSTACKS

When Giant Haystacks was staying at a hotel in Trinidad in 1982, his bed collapsed under his weight. A new one was brought, but when Giant Haystacks sat upon it its leg went straight through the floor and stuck through the ceiling of the breakfast room below. Giant Haystacks estimates that he spends about £1,500 on beds every year, buying a new one every three months. 'It's a touchy subject with my wife Rita,' he says. 'I've broken more beds than most people have had hot dinners.'

## *10 Sportsmen who* **Collect** *Things*

1 **Mick McManus** collects Meissen and Dresden china.

2 **Martina Navratilova** collects Art Deco. She particularly goes for

small bronze or marble statuettes of women throwing javelins or using bows and arrows.

3 **Adrian Street** collects model soldiers. He likes re-staging battles with them.

4 **Phil Hill** collects vintage cars and player piano rolls.

5 **Richie Gunther** collects antique pistols and Indian artefacts.

6 **Geoff Capes** collects prize-winning budgerigars.

7 **Tony Ward** collects soccer programmes. He has collected every one of England's home international programmes since 1947, and every Cup Final programme since 1955.

8 **Marvin Hagler** collects pigeons. He has over seventy.

9 **Bjorn Borg** collects islands. He has one near Stockholm and ten in the Baltic.

10 **Mike Brearley** collects his own dreams. He writes them down each morning in a log book which he keeps by the side of his bed.

## 7 Reasons why *Sportsmen have Complained*

### 1 A CHUMMY REFEREE
In November 1982, a number of local London soccer players complained to the Football Association that referee Janet Walmsley was stripping off and jumping in to bathe with the boys at the end of the games. 'I don't know why anyone should have complained,' retorted Miss Walmsley. 'I usually keep my knickers on. Sex is the last thing on my mind after reffing a game for ninety minutes.'

### 2 A TELEVISION DOCUMENTARY
After a documentary on The Stable Lads Welfare Trust had been screened on BBC2 in December 1982, journalist and racing commentator Peter O'Sullevan, a trustee of the charity, refused to attend the

BBC Sports Personality of the Year show. 'The film team showed at best, in my opinion, a gutter sense of integrity,' he complained.

### 3 SNORING
In November 1982 on the England cricket tour of Australia, Derek Randall and Eddie Hemmings had to be installed in the same room after complaints from their original room-mates that they snored too much.

### 4 A TELEVISION COMEDY SKETCH
In January 1982, Olly Croft, the seventeen-stone General Secretary of the British Darts Organization, complained about a sketch on the *Not The Nine O'Clock News* comedy programme, in which darts players had been portrayed pouring drink down their shirts and throats. 'We have worked hard to lose the cloth cap image. That sketch has set us back,' he said.

### 5 SOME MISSING TROPHIES
In June 1982, John McEnroe complained that he still hadn't been sent his trophies from the previous year's Wimbledon. Liaison officer Teddy Tinling countered: 'They were taken to the ball but he didn't turn up. They're still under lock and key in the secretary's office and we're longing to get rid of them.'

### 6 THE DRAUGHT
At the Moscow Olympics in 1980, the Finnish javelin throwers complained that the giant doors of the Olympic stadium were opened whenever a Russian was competing, thus giving helpful extra draught, and closed when they were competing.

### 7 SAFETY MEASURES
In 1974, Barry Sheene complained about the inadequate safety precautions on the Nurburgring racing circuit. 'You would have to be William Tell to hit a straw bale around here,' he said.

## 4 Reasons why people have **Complained about Sportsmen**

### 1 STEALING A GIRL
In December 1972, a disc jockey called Harry Murphy complained that Alex Higgins had stolen his fiancée, Linda Hughes, only a week before their wedding. Higgins had met Linda Hughes when he was playing an exhibition match in Glasgow. Higgins refuted Murphy's claims, saying, 'Miss Hughes said she wanted to see a bit of the country, so I offered her a job. She can drive me around and act as my assistant.'

### 2 SEVERING A PARTNERSHIP
On 27 January 1977, Gillian Gilks was accused of 'rank bad manners' by her doubles partner, Barbara Giles, after they had lost the Hearts of Oak Doubles title at Crystal Palace. Strife had arisen because Miss Gilks had decided to end her partnership with Essex secretary Miss Giles, after having won the All England, English national and Swedish titles all within the space of a year. Miss Giles vowed never again to speak to Miss Gilks.

### 3 GENERAL SLOPPINESS
Before presenting Trevor Francis with a trophy in the ATV Midland Soccer Awards, Brian Clough, said to him, 'You'll get nothing from me until you take your hands out of your pockets.'

### 4 JUST ONE THING
Interviewed four months after she had been married to Mark Spitz, his wife said that her only complaint about him was that he squeezed the toothpaste from the middle of the tube.

## 11 Sporting **Compliments**

1 **'He's racing's answer to William Shakespeare.'**
*Barry Brogan on David Gandolfo, trainer.*

2 **'I don't know what it is, but I take stuff from him I'd clip other guys in the ear for.'**
*Ian Botham on Mike Brearley.*

3 **'They should send Borg away to another planet. We play tennis. He plays something else.'**
*Ilie Nastase on Bjorn Borg.*

4 **'He goes out on the cricket square and doesn't give a bugger what the critics are saying. He just gets his head down and bats ... he's a good 'un.'**
*Harvey Smith on Geoff Boycott.*

5 **'I have only to think about Archie Gemmill to realize nothing is impossible in football.'**
*Peter Taylor on Archie Gemmill.*

6 **'Joe Louis was my inspiration. I idolized him. I just give lip service to being the greatest. He was the greatest.'**
*Muhammad Ali on Joe Louis, after Louis's death in 1981.*

7 **'He's the best rider who ever got on a horse anywhere, any time.'**
*Harry Carr on Lester Piggott.*

8 **'He is a sportsman and gentleman, on the court and beyond.'**
*Bjorn Borg on Ivan Lendl.*

9 **'There's so much class in our boardroom that some of them call the Queen "mate".'**
*Lawrie McMenemy on his directors.*

10 **'This Marvin Hagler – he's the Master of Disaster.'**
*Tony Sibson on Marvin Hagler (said when Tony Sibson had received seventeen stitches after lasting six rounds with Hagler in 1983. 'The Master of Disaster? Did he say that?' asked Hagler. 'Yeah, I think he's right.').*

11 **'He was a genius. He would walk down the yard at night with his little stick under his arm and all the horses would stand to attention.'**
*Sir Gordon Richards on Fred Darling.*

## 6 Sportsmen who Wear **Contact Lenses**

1 Jonah Barrington
2 Mark Phillips
3 Geoffrey Boycott
4 Derek Pringle
5 Fred Davis
6 Chris Tavaré

## 8 Sportsmen who have Participated in Bizarre **Contests**

### 1 DALEY THOMPSON TAKES ON A GREYHOUND
To raise money for the Olympic appeal for the 1980 Moscow Games, Daley Thompson raced the greyhound Autumn Groves at the Wimbledon dog track. Thompson ran 290 metres in 29 seconds but the handicapped greyhound ran a longer distance in a shorter time. 'One more leg and I would have beaten him,' he commented later.

### 2 IAN BOTHAM RIDES AGAINST DENNIS LILLEE
At Adelaide's Globe Derby Raceway in January 1983, Ian Botham rode So Sensitive to a three-yard victory over Dennis Lillee on Beau Lincoln in a special trotting race. Botham donated his $500 prize money to a charity for crippled children.

### 3 ALEX HIGGINS TAKES ON OLIVER REED
As a guest at Oliver Reed's home outside Dorking, in Surrey, Alex Higgins had to play his host at snooker, table tennis, arm wrestling and non-stop disco-dancing, with two pounds on each event.

### 4 JEFF THOMSON TAKES ON EGGS
In 1972, Jeff Thomson attempted to get into the *Guinness Book of Records* by beating the egg-throwing record. He failed in his quest because he couldn't work out a method by which eggs thrown over a long distance would remain intact when they landed in his hands.

### 5 JIMMY GREAVES CAMEL RACES V. BOB CHAMPION
In November 1982, Jimmy Greaves beat Bob Champion in a 100-yard camel race at a charity greyhound meeting in Crayford.

## 6 Billie Jean King takes on Bobby Riggs

In September 1973, Billie Jean King challenged the 1939 Wimbledon champion, Bobby Riggs, a sworn anti-feminist, to a tennis match at the Houston astrodome. Billie Jean King arrived sitting on a gold litter borne by male athletes, and Bobby Riggs arrived dressed up as King Henry VIII, sitting on a rickshaw drawn by female models, gnawing a bone and leering at a photograph of a naked woman. Before the match, Billie Jean King presented Bobby Riggs with a live pig, and in return he gave her a six-foot lollipop, saying, 'You're gonna be a sucker for my lobs.'

Billie Jean King won 6–4, 6–3, 6–3, and went away with the $100,000 prize money. But Riggs was unrepentant. 'I'll put Billie Jean and all the other women's libbers back where they belong – in the kitchen and the bedroom,' he said.

## 7 Alex Higgins takes on Suzi Quatro

In May 1973, Suzi Quatro challenged Alex Higgins to a £400 snooker match over five frames. Higgins won 79–45, 125–13 and 115–5.

'I'd take on any girl – at anything,' quipped Alex Higgins.

'I'm not doing this for publicity,' commented Suzi Quatro.

## 8 Alan Evans takes on Muhammad Ali

In South Shields in 1977, Alan Evans played a game of darts with Muhammad Ali, with Evans scoring only on trebles. Ali won, having managed to gain a bullseye along the way. He then proclaimed himself the Darts Champion of the World.

### *Henry Cooper's* 5 Most Difficult Opponents

1  Zora Folley
2  Alex Miteff
3  Floyd Patterson
4  Boston Jacobs
5  Muhammad Ali

*How Much it would **Cost** you to become a Sports Patron*

**Staging the Olympics** would cost you anything between £200,000,000 (Moscow 1980) and £800,000,000 (Montreal 1976).

**Staging the World Cup** would cost a minimum of £85,000,000 (Spain 1982).

**Persuading John McEnroe to play with your tennis racquets for a year** would cost you £300,000 (but Dunlop have already persuaded him).

**Persuading Steve Davis to make forty personal appearances** would cost you £220,000 (but John Courage have already paid him that for a three-year period which began in January 1982).

**Buying a Formula One engine** would cost you over £25,000 (but be warned: you can only use it for one race).

**Buying a champion racing pigeon** would cost you about £10,500 (the price De Blicksen was sold for in 1975).

**Keeping and training a horse** would cost you an absolute minimum of £6,000 a year.

**Buying a set of dentures like Jocky Wilson's** would cost you £1,200, which is what they cost him in May 1982.

**Hiring a top-class soccer referee** would cost you £40 a match.

**Hiring a jump jockey** would cost you £32.50 a ride, plus 7½% of any winnings.

**Hiring a caddy** would cost you £20 a day, plus up to 5% of any winnings.

## English **County Cricket** Champions since 1972

1972 Warwickshire
1973 Hampshire
1974 Worcestershire
1975 Leicestershire
1976 Middlesex
1977 Middlesex and Kent
1978 Kent
1979 Essex
1980 Middlesex
1981 Nottinghamshire
1982 Middlesex

## 10 English **County Cricketers** who Bat Right-handed and Bowl Left-handed

1 John Lever (*Essex and England*)
2 Derek Underwood (*Kent and England*)
3 Phillipe Edmonds (*Middlesex and England*)
4 Dennis Amiss (*Warwickshire and England*)
5 David Hughes (*Lancashire*)
6 Ray East (*Essex*)
7 Nick Pocock (*Hampshire*)
8 David Graveney (*Gloucestershire*)
9 Nick Cook (*Leicestershire*)
10 Geoff Cook (*Northants and England*)

CRIED

## 7 Sportsmen who have **Cried**

1 BRIAN CLOUGH
Brian Clough cried when he failed his eleven-plus.

2 JOCKY WILSON
Jocky Wilson cried when he won the Embassy World Darts Championship in January 1982. 'Jocky is an emotional lad', said organizer Olly Croft.

3 JACK NICKLAUS
Having won his first Open at Muirfield in 1966, Jack Nicklaus said, 'Excuse me, friends, do you mind if I weep? You see I just want to enjoy this moment.' Then he burst into tears.

4 DUNCAN GOODHEW
Duncan Goodhew used to cry when asked to read out loud in his junior school. He had dyslexia.

5 SILVANO MARTINA
In November 1981, World Cup star Giancarlo Antognoni's heart stopped for twenty-five seconds after goalkeeper Silvano Martina's knee had caught him in the head during an Italian League match. 'When I saw Antognoni lying in that condition, I cried like a baby,' Martina confessed. 'I've never wanted to harm anyone.' Happily, Antognoni revived after the kiss of life had been administered.

6 JOSH GIFFORD
Josh Gifford wept when Bob Champion won the Grand National on Aldaniti. But Champion's eyes remained dry. 'I didn't have time to weep,' he said, 'I had to go and ride in another race.'

7 LAWRIE MCMENEMY
When Southampton were beaten by Burnley, leading to Southampton's relegation to the Second Division, Lawrie McMenemy cried in his hotel room. He also cried when he was sacked from Doncaster Rovers in May 1971. He had a wife and three children to support, and no money.

## 5 Sportsmen who have **Criticized** the critics

### 1 LEE TREVINO
'They say, "Trevino is wondering whether to play a five or six iron to the green", when all the time I'm gazing at some broad in the third row of the gallery and wondering where the hell my wife is.'

### 2 GEOFFREY BOYCOTT
'Henry Blofeld is frequently long on opinions and short on facts.'

### 3 MUHAMMAD ALI
'Look, I tried to tell you how great I was but you chumps wouldn't listen.' (To reporters after he had beaten Sonny Liston.)

### 4 MAX RAFFERTY, CALIFORNIAN STATE SUPERINTENDENT OF PUBLIC INSTRUCTION
'Critics of college football are kooks, crumbums and commies, hairy loudmouth beatniks.'

### 5 CRAIG STADLER
'I wish they would start talking about the quality of my golf, not my wardrobe; print my score, not my measurements.'


## 5 Notable **Cross-Channel** Swims

### 1 JABEZ WOLFFE
Between 1906 and 1914, Jabez Wolffe made twenty-two attempts to swim the English Channel. He never once managed to reach England.

### 2 EMAKU GLUCO
In 1920, an Eskimo called Emaku Gluco attempted to swim the twenty-one miles of the Catalina Strait between the Californian coast and the island of Santa Catalina. He trained for the attempt by living in a refrigerator and eating only walrus meat and blubber specially shipped to him from the Arctic. But halfway across he abandoned the attempt, complaining bitterly that the water was too warm.

### 3 FOUR BLIND MEN

On 10 August 1969, a team of four blind men swam in relay from France to Folkestone in fourteen hours and thirty-eight minutes. They were guided by pop music from a transistor radio on their pilot boat.

### 4 TED MAY

In 1954, Ted May, a 44-year-old Birmingham steelworker, attempted to swim the English Channel towing behind himself a small raft containing two bottles of rum. After nine hours he gave up. A second attempt ended in his death.

### 5 SHIRLEY MAY FRANCE

In September 1949, a 17-year-old American schoolgirl called Shirley May France attempted to swim the English Channel. The Hollywood film producer Edward Small had promised her a film contract if she succeeded, but after ten hours and forty-two minutes her father ordered her out of the water a clear seven miles from the British coast. Little is known of her subsequent film career, if indeed she had one.

# D

*Dirty **Darts** – 6 Tips from an Anonymous Professional on How to Put your Opponent Off*

1 RATTLING
At strategic moments, rattle your darts together as your opponent is taking aim.

2 TALKING
Chat away, on any topic, to anyone, including your opponent.

3 LAGGING
When your opponent is keen to get on with his go, take an especially long time extracting your darts from the board.

4 SMOKING
Form a smoke screen by blowing cigarette smoke between your opponent and the board.

5 IMPEDING
Once you have extracted your darts, walk straight towards your opponent rather than moving to one side.

6 COMPLAINING
Complain about anything at any time, thus stopping the flow of play.

*4 Ways in which **Steve Davis** Relaxes*

1 He reads Tom Sharpe and John Le Carré novels.
2 He plays Space Invaders.
3 He plays mental chess.
4 He accompanies his car's cassette recorder with his own harmonica.

## 7 Notable **Dead Heats**

### 1 FOUR RUNNERS

In the 1952 Helsinki Olympics, four men were credited with the same time, of 10.4 seconds, in the 100 metres final. They were Lindy Remingo (USA), Herb McKenley (Jamaica), McDonald Bailey (GB), and Dean Smith (USA). Judges awarded the race to Remingo. McKenley, who was second, considered that he had won, but added, 'I don't want to win on protest, or on a photograph. I want to win on my legs.'

### 2 TWO JOCKEYS

The 1981–82 National Hunt Jockey Championship was shared between John Francome and Peter Scudamore. This was partly due to the decency of Francome. Scudamore had been injured late in the season and Francome kept riding until he had drawn equal with him and then refused to ride any more. 'Peter has worked really hard and deserves to be champion,' he said.

### 3 FOUR HORSES

In April 1951, in the Omnibus Stakes at The Hoo, the first recorded example of a quadruple dead heat occurred. The Defaulter, Squire of Malton, Pulcherrima and Reindeer all crossed the finishing line at the same time.

### 4 TWO CRICKET TEAMS

In the First Test at Brisbane in 1960, Australia had three wickets left and eight balls in which to score six runs. On the first ball, a single run was scored. On the second ball, Benaud was caught out. On the third ball, nothing happened. On the fourth ball, there was a bye. On the fifth ball, there was a single run. There were now three balls left and three runs needed. On the sixth ball, Meckiff hit the ball towards the boundary, but as they were going for the third run Wally Grout was run out. Now Australia needed one run, and the West Indies needed one wicket. As Meckiff set out to take a run, Joe Solomon's throw hit the wicket. The game was the only tie in Test cricket history. Benaud, the Australian captain, said later, 'It was the greatest match I have ever played in and the finish was fantastic.'

### 5 TWO BRITISH RUNNERS

In the Commonwealth Games in October 1982, Allan Wells and Mike

Macfarlane dead-heated in the 200 metres. This is the only recorded dead heat in a major athletics competition.

## 6 TWO FOREIGN RUNNERS
In the Wanamaker Mile of 1950, both Fred Wilt and Don Gehrmann were timed at 4.09.3. After a debate lasting a full eleven months, Gehrmann was declared winner.

## 7 FIVE HORSES
In August 1880, in the Astley stakes at Lewes, Mazurka, Scobell, Wandering Nun, Cumberland and Thora all seemed to have crossed the line together. Eventually, it was decided that the first three had dead-heated for first place and the last two had come joint fourth.

*... and one Motorcyclist who just Missed a Dead Heat ...*

In the 1979 Marlboro British Grand Prix at Silverstone, Barry Sheene lost to Kenny Roberts by three hundredths of a second, or the rim of a wheel.

## The 10 **Decathlon** Events

| First Day | Second Day |
|---|---|
| 100 Metres | 100 Metres Hurdles |
| Long Jump | Discus |
| Shot Putt | Pole Vault |
| High Jump | Javelin |
| 400 Metres | 1500 Metres |

## 7 Things which have Influenced Sporting **Departures**

### 1 BUDDHA
On the Saturday before he announced his retirement in January 1983, Bjorn Borg prayed for guidance in a Buddhist temple in Bangkok. He came out believing that the gods had released him from tennis.

## 2 THE HUSBAND

Jo Champion, the wife of Bob Champion, gave up steeplechasing and took to flat racing in the summer of 1982. This was at the request of her husband.

## 3 THE WIFE

When Sugar Ray Leonard retired from boxing in 1982, his wife Judy said, 'I just told him that if he didn't quit I'd break his fingers.'

## 4 GOD

Nine months after becoming a Jehova's Witness in 1969, Wolves footballer Peter Knowles gave up soccer to become an unpaid evangelist. 'If you were on a football field and I had to stop you scoring a goal, I would not hesitate to kick you. And that's not Christian,' he explained.

## 5 THE MANAGER'S ENTHUSIASM

After Tommy Docherty had been appointed the manager of Chelsea, a player went to him and said, 'I've got a shock for you – I want a transfer.'

'I've got a shock for you, too,' replied Docherty. 'You can have one.'

## 6 PHILANTHROPY

Announcing his retirement from swimming in September 1973, Mark Spitz said that he was devoting his life to the State of Israel, the problems of mental illness and the physically handicapped. He added that he had been helped in his decision by his wife Susan.

## 7 ONE OF TWO REASONS

On 11 July 1977, Don Revie resigned as manager of the English football team. 'I sat down with my wife Elsie and we agreed that the job was no longer worth the aggravation,' he explained.

On 12 July, the *Daily Mail*, revealed that Don Revie had accepted a job in the United Arab Emirates at a salary of £60,000 a year.

## 4 Sporting **Diabetics**

1 Billie Jean King, *tennis player*
2 Gary Mabbutt, *footballer*
3 Danny McGrain, *footballer*
4 Warren Simpson, *snooker player* (died 1980)

## **Michael Dickinson's** First 5 Home

On 17 March 1983, 33-year-old trainer Michael Dickinson achieved the unique record of training the first five horses past the post in the Cheltenham Gold Cup. The horses were:

> 1st: Bregawn (100–30)
> 2nd: Captain John (11–1)
> 3rd: Wayward Lad (6–1)
> 4th: Silver Buck (5–1)
> 5th: Ashley House (12–1)

After the race, Dickinson said, 'It's been hell. If only the public knew what a responsibility it has been. I feel drained rather than elated.'

## 11 People who have **Died** while Playing Sport

### 1 HENRY HIGGINS
The English bullfighter Henry Higgins was killed in 1978 when his hang-glider crashed to the ground after he had jumped from a 200 foot high hill near Moscar in South-East Spain.

### 2 VLADIMIR SMIRNOV
During a fencing bout in Italy in 1982, Olympic Gold Medallist Vladimir Smirnov was pierced in the eye and died without regaining consciousness.

# DIED

## 3 BOBBY BENSON
Bobby Benson, a Sheffield United full-back who played one game for England in 1913, was persuaded to return to play for Arsenal against Reading after a year's retirement. Halfway through the game he left feeling ill, and he died in the changing room, aged thirty-three.

## 4 ALEX AGAR
In 1884, on the Randwick racetrack in Australia, bare-knuckle fighter James Lawson of Sydney hit Alex Agar of Melbourne just above the left eye. Agar arrived dead at a Sydney hospital. Lawson was sent to prison for manslaughter, and bare-knuckle fighting was banned thereafter.

## 5 FREDERICK, PRINCE OF WALES
Frederick, Prince of Wales, died in 1751 from a blow from a cricket ball.

## 6 RENATO CURI
In May 1977, Renato Curi, the 24-year-old midfield star of Italian First Division club Perugia, died of a heart attack after colliding with another player. Three doctors who had examined him before the match were later prosecuted for negligence. It was alleged that they should have forbidden him to play.

## 7 RUDOLF ROY
In July 1971, at a Montreal golf course, Rudolf Roy, aged forty-three, was killed when his club snapped, rebounded off a tree, and entered his heart.

## 8 HYACINTHUS
The Greek god Apollo killed his boyfriend Hyacinthus accidentally while practising his discus throwing.

## 9 JOHN THOMPSON
In September 1931 at Ibrox Park, the 22-year-old Celtic goalkeeper John Thompson dived at the feet of Rangers centre-forward Sam English, fractured his skull and died five hours later.

## 10 WILLIAM DE SPALDING
In 1322, William de Spalding, a Gilbertine Canon from Shouldham in Norfolk, accidentally killed a friend while playing football with an

unsheathed knife. After hearing all the evidence, Pope John XXII absolved him of all blame.

## 11 PHILIPPIDES

The founder of the Marathon. When the Persians invaded Greece in 490 BC, the Athenians, hopelessly outnumbered, despatched a runner, Philippides, to Sparta to appeal for help. Philippides covered the 150 miles in two days. Unfortunately the Spartans were otherwise engaged, and upon his return the brave runner collapsed from exhaustion and died.

## The Daily *Diet* of Pakistani Wrestler Akram Bholoo

1 Four Chickens
2 Ten pints of milk
3 Five pounds of dried fruit
4 (Weekly) An entire roast goat

## 13 Peculiar *Diets* of Sportsmen

### 1 THREE RAW EGGS IN A GLASS OF BEER

The daily drink of Leon Spinks, former World Heavyweight Champion.

### 2 GINSENG TEA WITH HONEY

The daily drink of Geoff Boycott. He acknowledges his debt to Barbara Cartland in the shaping of his dietary requirements.

### 3 CHEESE AND MARMITE SANDWICHES

Enjoyed for breakfast by Steve Davis.

### 4 SPONGE CAKE AND CHAMPAGNE

The favourite food and drink of Lucy Walker (1836–1916). She was the first woman to climb the Matterhorn. She would climb in a white print dress and eat sponge cake and drink champagne along the way.

### 5 GUNPOWDER AND WARM BLOOD
An American umpire once said of the notoriously violent Baltimore Orioles that they 'breakfasted on gunpowder and warm blood'.

### 6 PRACTICALLY NOTHING
John Francome has a crash-course diet which lasts a fortnight and loses him twelve pounds. It consists of a bowl of cereal or a half a grapefruit for breakfast, two ounces of meat and salad for lunch, and the same for supper with a piece of fruit. His only drink is black coffee.

### 7 CHAMPAGNE AND LOBSTERS
Somerset cricketer Sammy Woods used to drink champagne and eat lobsters for breakfast.

### 8 NO SALADS
Babe Ruth always refused salads. 'Asparagus makes my urine smell,' he would complain.

### 9 NO RED MEAT
Billie Jean King does not eat red meat. She also avoids white sugar and food made with white flour.

### 10 FROGS' HEADS
In 1977, a school coach was ordered by the American Humane Association to stop biting the heads off frogs during his pep talks before each football game.

### 11 ONE MARS BAR
In 1979, after the horse No Bombs had won a £4,000 race at Worcester by eight lengths, crossing the line at a canter, he was tested for dope, and a urine sample was found to contain caffeine. A Jockey Club inquiry heard from trainer Peter Easterby that No Bombs had eaten some of a stable lad's Mars Bar while travelling to the race. Further tests proved the truth of this, and the Jockey Club was satisfied. Nevertheless, No Bombs was disqualified and lost the prize money.

### 12 SHERRY WELL DASHED WITH WATER, RAW OYSTERS, STRONG BEEF TEA, CELERY, CALF-FOOT JELLY AND A SMALL PORTION OF BOILED CHICKEN
The diet of 'Professor' William Miller, who in 1879 walked 102 miles in 24 hours.

13 STRAWBERRY MILK SHAKES
Ian Botham enjoys strawberry milk shakes for breakfast.

## What 5 Sportsmen Think of being **Disliked** by Millions

1 'You don't go to an X-rated movie if you don't want to watch it.'
*Ilie Nastase, after television viewers had complained about his language, December 1981.*

2 'I'm the Nastase of golf. If golf didn't have a player like me it would be a dreary sport.'
*Tom Weiskopf.*

3 'It's got to the stage where I'm beginning to come out like a cross between Attila the Hun and Ghengis Khan, and I wouldn't like kids coming into the sport to think that you have to be mean to get on.'
*Steve Ovett.*

4 'If you all hate Bristow clap your hands.'
*Eric Bristow's old way of starting off exhibition matches.*

5 'When he was in the ring, everybody booooooed and booooooed. Oh, everybody just booooooooed. And I was mad. And I looked around and I saw everybody was mad. I saw 15,000 people coming to see this man get beat. And I said, this is a goooood idea.'
*Muhammad Ali, describing going to see the white wrestler Gorgeous George as a young man.*

## 5 Reasons for **Disqualification**

1 A PRACTICE PUTT
In the 1937 New Zealand Open Championship, A. Murray made a practice putt at the eighth hole in the last round. For this he was disqualified. But for that, he would have won.

## 2 A DEVIOUS CADDY

In the first round of the PGA championship in 1968, Maurice Bembridge was disqualified after his caddie had pretended to find his ball in the rough. Unaware that it wasn't really his ball, Bembridge played it, only to discover the real ball a few yards on. Bembridge was disqualified and his caddy was sacked.

## 3 WALKING OFF

At the 1920 Antwerp Olympics, in the soccer final, the Czech team walked off in protest at the behaviour of the crowd, who were constantly booing their home team, believing that not enough local players had been included. For walking off, the Czechs were disqualified.

## 4 NUDITY

Running in a 5,000 metre race at the Erith Athletic ground in 1971, David Bedford was alerted by his club that he was wearing only a plain vest and not the required club vest. While still running he changed vests and then he went on to win. But he was disqualified on two counts – for wearing incorrect apparel and for baring his back to all eight people in the crowd.

## 5 IMPUNCTUALITY

Sevvy Ballesteros was disqualified from the 1980 US Open Championship when he arrived at the first tee ten minutes late.

*The 8 Cricketers who have scored **Double Centuries** in Tests at Lord's*

| | | | |
|---|---|---|---|
| 1 | Sir Donald Bradman (*Aus.*) | 254 | *against* England in 1930 |
| 2 | Bill Brown (*Aus.*) | 206 | *against* England in 1938 |
| 3 | Denis Compton (*Eng.*) | 208 | *against* South Africa in 1947 |
| 4 | Martin Donnelly (*NZ*) | 206 | *against* England in 1949 |
| 5 | Walter Hammond (*Eng.*) | 240 | *against* Australia in 1938 |
| 6 | Joe Hardstaff (*Eng.*) | 205 | *against* India in 1946 |
| 7 | Sir Jack Hobbs (*Eng.*) | 211 | *against* South Africa in 1924 |
| 8 | Mohsin Khan (*Pak.*) | 200 | *against* England in 1982 |

## *Derek Dougan's* 5 Reasons for the Crisis in Football

1 Hooliganism
2 Over-pricing
3 Lack of community involvement
4 The effect of the recession
5 Greater competition

## *Derek Dougan's* 5 Suggestions for How to Get Football out of the Crisis

1 Stronger sentences against serious offenders – but above all an involvement by the clubs themselves with their own supporters.
2 A return to half-price for children and senior citizens; free or reduced admission for the unemployed, provided a means could be found to do this with dignity – which does not mean entrances at a specific turnstile.
3 The clubs have become too remote from the community. This is the fault of clubs at every level of football, and not just individuals. The supporters must feel they belong.
4 End the recession!
5 Inevitably, more leisure time has produced more reasons for spending surplus cash on entertainment, viz golf is a classless sport now, and the same with tennis, badminton, squash, etc. Also, of course, the enormous pull of television and video means that we must devise better ways of encouraging families in particular to come back to watch live football. There is no infallible cure. It is very much a question of finding the right formula by trial and error.

## 4 Sports which have Gone **Downhill**

1 MOTOR RACING
'In my day it was 75% car and mechanics, 25% driver and luck. Today it is 95% car. A driver can emerge in a good new car, become

world champion and a year later disappear to the back of the queue. Driving skill hardly counts any more.'

*Juan Manuel Fangio, aged 72, winner of 24 grand prix and 5 world champion-ships.*

## 2 TENNIS
'What saddens me about some young players is not merely that they lack devotion to the history of the game but that they have little curiosity about anything around them.'

*Billie Jean King.*

## 3 CRICKET
'It is pretty certain that if I were young today, I wouldn't become devoted to first-class cricket and wish to write about it. ... Since around about 1960, cricket, in the organized form in which it is presented to the public, has been changed so much that W.G. Grace would not know it was cricket at all.'

*Sir Neville Cardus.*

## 4 APRES-SKI SPORT
'Before, one went into the Palace Bar between six and eight and everyone was there. One met up with a girl one had seen on the slopes, and one took it from there. Now you meet the girl on the ski-lift and miss out the drinks. It's just, "Your room or mine?" to which she is likely to reply, "If you're going to make a problem out of it, let's forget it".'

*Hans Jorg Badrutt.*

## 5 TENNIS AGAIN
'Tennis has changed; come into money and absolutely gone public. One walks about in the players' enclosure trying to get tea, and hearing things like "contracts", "franchises", "legal representatives" and "twelve point five million by May". It's the day of the superstar, the supercoach, the how-to books, the tennis universities and the tracksuits with the stripes down the side.'

*Gordon Forbes, former tennis pro.*

## The 5 **Dreams** of Lord Kilbracken

As an undergraduate at Oxford University, John Godley, later Lord Kilbracken, had the first of many dreams which would win him a fortune ...

1 His first dream involved him seeing the racing results in the next day's paper. On the strength of this dream, he backed two winners at 9-2 and 10-1.

2 Back home in Ireland, he had another dream and backed the horse, which won at 100-6.

3 Back in Oxford he dreamt that he was phoning his bookie to discover the winner of the last race and was told 'Monumental at 5-4.' There was in fact no horse called Monumental, but there was a horse called Mentores. Kilbracken backed it and it won at 5-4.

4 In 1947, when newspapers were beginning to take an interest in him, he dreamt that the crowd were shouting for 'The Bogey' in the 4.30. There was no horse called The Bogey, but there was a horse called The Brogue, and he phoned the *Daily Mirror* before the race telling them that it would win. It did win, and he was immediately offered a job on the *Daily Mirror*.

5 Alas, Kilbracken's dreams did not enjoy their new professional status, and most of the horses they suggested turned out to be losers. But in Monte Carlo, in 1958, he dreamt that What Man would win the Grand National as third favourite. He placed £25 on a horse called Mr What and it won at 18-1.

## 9 Sportsmen who have been Affected by **Drink**

1 JOCKY WILSON
In October 1982, Jocky Wilson missed when attempting to shake hands with his opponent. 'A wonderful talent will be wasted unless we can rectify this drink problem,' said his manager, Ron Clover.

2 DORARDO PIETRI
After Dorardo Pietri's collapse in the stadium as he was winning the 1908 London Olympic Marathon, it was rumoured that he had been

gargling with Chantilly whilst he was running, and that his loss of any sense of direction, followed by his collapse, was brought about as much by wine as by exhaustion.

### 3 JIMMY GREAVES

A self-confessed alcoholic, Jimmy Greaves' autobiography includes chapters entitled 'I am an Alcoholic', 'The First Drop' and 'Drinking for England'. At publication he said that any money he made from the book would be taken by the Inland Revenue, 'to clear debts that mounted while I was hitting the bottle'.

### 4 RANDOLPH LYCETT

Randolph Lycett, the Australian winner of the men's doubles at Wimbledon in 1921, 1922 and 1923, was served champagne by a liveried waiter in between games at Wimbledon in 1920. After his defeat in the singles, he had to be carried off court.

### 5 GEORGE BEST

Joining Alcoholics Anonymous in February 1980, George Best described two-bottles-a-day Jimmy Greaves as 'only a starter'.

### 6 THE NEW BRADWELL ST PETER'S FOOTBALL TEAM

In January 1983, when the New Bradwell St Peter's football team, Milton Keynes, were knocked from their top position on a local league table, their manager Malcolm Burridge blamed the defeat on a heavy celebration the night before. 'It was a shambles,' he said. 'Six of them were still drunk. Their places are in jeopardy.'

### 7 ABD-EL KADER ZAAG

In 1950, in the middle of the Perpignan–Nimes stage of the Tour de France, North African cyclist Abd-El Kader Zaag was overcome by the temperature, which was in the nineties, and accepted a bottle of wine from a spectator. He drank the whole bottle and a few minutes later tumbled off his bike. After five minutes asleep he awoke, remounted his bike and pedalled away at top speed back in the direction from which he had come.

### 8 BARRY BROGAN

Barry Brogan claims to have spent £750 on alcohol in one fortnight in Greece. He later joined Alcoholics Anonymous, which he described as 'My only hope, the only barrier between life and doom.'

## 9 A.P. BAILEY

In 1908, A.P. Bailey, the Leicester Fosse goalkeeper, let in twelve goals in one game against Nottingham Forest, although playing in five games for England he had only let in three goals. A Football League committee accused him of accepting bribes, but acquitted him after hearing his argument that he had still not recovered from a colleague's wedding two days previously.

*. . . and one Sportsman who Swears he isn't Affected by Drink*

'I need six pints to get to the table, even for a practice,' admits Bill Werbeniuk. 'Then I need a pint for every frame. In a long day I can get through twenty-five to thirty pints.'

He insists, though, that, 'Fortunately, I have a good capacity for drink and it doesn't make me tipsy.'

## *4 Darts Players' Ideas about* **Drink**

### 1 ERIC BRISTOW
'Sometimes, during a really tense match, I can sink a pint in one swallow. I don't know I'm doing it.'

### 2 BOBBY GEORGE
'I learnt to play darts before I learnt to drink. For some players, darts and booze are linked. It's psychological.'

### 3 JOCKY WILSON
'I need seven or eight vodkas to keep my nerves in the proper state so that I can play at my best.'

### 4 ALAN EVANS
'I like to get four pints down me before a game. Then I always take another with me when I go up to play. I like strong dry cider best, but you can't always get it in some clubs, so then I settle for beer.'

## 5 **Drugs** which have Killed Sportsmen

### 1 AMPHETAMINES
On 24 October 1972, Jean-Louis Quadri, an 18-year-old French soccer player, collapsed on the field as he was about to shoot for goal. At the autopsy, a high level of amphetamines was found in his blood stream.

### 2 METHYLAMPHETAMINE
During the 1967 Tour de France, Tom Simpson, a British cyclist, collapsed and died. Methylamphetamine, amphetamine and cognac were all found in his body. In 1965 he had been world champion.

### 3 HEROIN
New York welterweight boxer Billy Bello died of heroin poisoning in 1963. Dick Howard, the American who came third in the 400 metres hurdles in the 1960 Olympics, also died of heroin poisoning.

### 4 RONICOL
At the 1960 Rome Olympics, a young Danish cyclist called Knut Enemark Jensen died from the drug ronicol, which dilates the blood vessels.

### 5 TRIMETHYL
In the 1886 Bordeaux to Paris cycle race, Englishman John Linton died from an overdose of trimethyl given to him by his trainer.

# E

## 6 Causes of Sporting **Embarrassment**

### 1 INEFFICIENT KNICKER ELASTIC
As she was playing on Number 10 court at Wimbledon, Hazel Phillips' knicker elastic snapped. When she asked permission to leave the court to put on another pair, the referee, John Legge, at first refused. He quickly relented when he saw hundreds of press reporters and photographers flooding in.

### 2 THE WONDERS OF MODERN COMMUNICATION
Touring Australia in 1978-79, England fast bowler Mike Hendrick insisted to a radio interviewer that he wasn't homesick at all. A minute later, he was given a surprise introduction to his wife at the other end of the line.

### 3 A BREATHALYSER TEST
Lawrie McMenemy, who had been seen often on television commercials advertising an alcohol-free lager called Barbican, was breathalysed when police stopped him at Portswood, Southampton, in 1980.

### 4 FRAIL TROUSERS
In October 1980, eighteen-stone snooker player Bill Werbeniuk got up from his chair in a televised match to the sound of a great rip. His trousers had split. He said later, 'I never wear underpants. I've always found them very uncomfortable. It was a highly embarrassing moment.'

### 5 RESTLESS BOSOMS
Playing Billie Jean King at Wimbledon in 1979, Linda Siegal's bosoms popped out of the top of her dress. She hastily popped them back again.

### 6 A MODEST LAVATORY
When Giant Haystacks went to the loo in an aeroplane while travelling to Calcutta in 1978, he got stuck there. When the plane landed, he

was rescued by airport firemen who cut him free with a welding torch. 'I've never been so embarrassed in my life,' he commented.

## 7 *People who have been Less Than **Enthusiastic** about Sport*

### 1 RODNEY MARSH
Rodney Marsh once said, 'Soccer in England is a grey game, played on grey days, watched by grey people.'

### 2 GEORGE ORWELL
In 1950, George Orwell wrote, 'Serious sport has nothing to do with fair play. It is bound up with hatred, jealousy, boastfulness, disregard of all rules and sadistic pleasure in witnessing violence; in other words it is war minus the shooting.'

### 3 ASLAM SHER KHAN
The first Muslim to represent Pakistan at hockey, Aslam Sher Khan wrote a book called *To Hell With Hockey*. In it, he complained that 'Sport in India is a gravy train that catapults you to popularity.'

### 4 DR HARRY COOPER
When Charlotte Cooper won her first Ladies Singles title at Wimbledon in 1895, she cycled back to Surbiton, where she was staying with her brother, Dr Harry Cooper, and discovered him pruning roses in the garden.
'What have you been doing, Chattie?' he asked.
'I've just won the championship,' she replied.
Dr Cooper said nothing, and carried on pruning his roses.

### 5 SIR WINSTON CHURCHILL
Sir Winston once described golf as 'an ineffectual attempt to direct an uncontrollable sphere into an inaccessible hole with instruments ill-adapted to the purpose'.

### 6 ROSI MITTERMAIER
The German Gold Medal skier said in 1976, 'The main thing to

remember is not to take sport too seriously. I have learned that because I have been beaten too often.'

## 7 TOM WEISKOPF
In July 1982, Tom Weiskopf said, 'Golf has never been and never will be the most important part of my life.'

# F

*7 Sportsmen who have **Fallen Over***

**1 STEVE OVETT FALLS OUTSIDE A CHURCH**
In December 1981, Steve Ovett was passing a church on an early morning run when he glanced at details of a carol service on the noticeboard and slipped on to the church railings. He punctured a muscle over his knee and tore the inside of his leg.

**2 ROBIN COUSINS FALLS ON THE PODIUM**
Having won the Men's Figure Skating competition in the 1980 Lake Placid Olympics, Robin Cousins tripped as he stepped on to the podium to receive his Gold Medal from Lord Killanin.

**3 JEAN BOITEUX'S FATHER FALLS INTO THE POOL**
Just after Jean Boiteux of France had won the 400 metres freestyle in the 1952 Helsinki Olympics, his father rushed up to congratulate him, slipped and plunged into the pool.

**4 ALL FALL AT THE 23RD**
In the 1967 Grand National all but one of the surviving runners were brought down or impeded at the 23rd fence, leaving 100–1 outsider Foinavon to win.

**5 JACK NICKLAUS FALLS ON TO THE HOSPITAL FLOOR**
Jack Nicklaus fainted as he watched the birth of his first child, Jack jr, in 1961. Nurses brought him round, at which point he was sick. He was also sick at the birth of each of his other children.

**6 GIANT HAYSTACKS FALLS IN THE RING**
Fighting in Kuwait in 1980, Giant Haystacks fell on his elbow and broke his ribcage. More trouble followed when he couldn't fit into the ambulance which had been called. He was eventually transported to a hospital in an open truck.

**7  CARMEN BROWN FALLS ON THE TRACK**
Competing in the notoriously overcrowded American Amateur Athletics Union Indoor Championships in February 1974, Carmen Brown was coming first in the women's sprint when a vaulter knocked a cross bar on to her track and she tripped over.


## 5  *Sportsmen who were* ***Falsely Accused***


**1  BOBBY MOORE**
In May 1970, shortly after arriving in Bogota for the World Cup, Bobby Moore was detained in police custody for four days. It was alleged that he had stolen an emerald bracelet worth £600. The bracelet had not been discovered on him, even though he had not left the vicinity of the shop before his arrest. The main witness, a Señor Suarez, was soon discovered to be involved in the blackmarket emerald trade. The case was dropped when Señor Suarez kept changing his evidence.


**2  JIMMY WHITE**
Snooker star Jimmy White and his wife were arrested for stealing a handbag during the Tooting riots of June 1981. They were later cleared. They had picked up a £23 handbag lying on the ground near the broken window of a shop when Special Patrol Group officers pounced on them. 'It's crazy that you can't walk along the street, see something on the pavement and pick it up out of curiosity without being arrested,' White remarked later.


**3  BOBBY GEORGE**
In January 1982, a television viewer noticed three rings on Bobby George's fingers and went to the police claiming that they were his. After an interview with the police, George was set free.


**4  GEORGE BEST**
In 1973, George Best was charged with stealing a fur coat, passport, chequebook and other items from his ex-girlfriend Marjorie Wallace. He was cleared and left the court, in the words of the judge, 'without a stain on his character'.

## 5 GARTH CROOKS

In June 1981, Garth Crooks was arrested after a woman told police that he had been present at a burglary of her Fulham house the previous night. Having kept him for an hour in custody, a police spokesman said, 'Garth was able to verify his movements and his identity. We released him with considerable apologies. It was clearly a case of mistaken identity. Garth took the whole thing very well. He was very understanding. I'm one of his fans now.'

### Christmas Day *Fancy Dress* Costumes of 11 Touring Cricketers

*(It is traditional for the English Cricket XI to wear Fancy Dress at their Christmas lunch.)*

1 Derek Randall: A Fairy Queen

2 David Gower: Pontius Pilate

3 Ken Barrington: An Indian

4 Graham Gooch: Oliver Twist

5 Geoff Boycott: Adam

6 Mike Brearley: A Galillean Greengrocer

7 Doug Insole: Inspector Clouseau

8 Geoff Miller: A Derbyshire Miner

9 John Emburey: A Green Lizard

10 Clive Radley: An Indian

11 Bob Willis: A Blind Umpire

## 8 Peculiar *Fan Letters* Sent to Sportsmen

### 1 TO SANDY LYLE WITH LOVE
After Sandy Lyle had been chosen to play for Britain in the Walker Cup in America, an elderly male fan sent him a cheque for £50 to buy chewing gum and chocolate while he was over there.

### 2 TO JOHN LLOYD WITH LOVE
John Lloyd once received a letter asking him to wear a headband if it would be all right to come to his hotel room after the match. It was written by a man.

### 3 TO KEITH DELLER WITH LOVE
When Keith Deller won the 1983 Embassy World Professional Darts Championship, a girl wrote to him saying that when he smiled he looked just like Dracula, and would he sink his teeth into her neck?

### 4 TO DEREK RANDALL WITH LOVE
After he had scored 174 runs in the Centenary Test Match at Melbourne in 1977, Derek Randall was sent 174 pork chops by a Nottingham butcher.

### 5 TO RED RUM WITH LOVE
In 1978, Red Rum received a letter from an eighteen-year-old girl, enclosing a cheque for £10 to buy himself some peppermints and in return asking for a signed photograph.

### 6 TO LAWRIE MCMENEMY WITH LOVE
In 1982, Lawrie McMenemy admitted, 'I get lots of letters from women – between the ages of eighty and a hundred. My wife has no problems on that score.'

### 7 TO ADRIAN STREET WITH LOVE
Wrestler Adrian Street once received a letter from a brothel in Hanover extending an open invitation to visit the ladies of the house – free.

### 8 TO JOHN MCENROE WITH LOVE
A Japanese fan once sent John McEnroe a doll of himself. His then girlfriend Stacey Margolin used to keep it by the side of her bed in Beverley Hills and punch it whenever she was cross with him.

## 15 Fanatical Sports **Fans**

### 1 SISTER COLLETTE DUVEEN
In June 1978, Sister Collette Duveen, a nun from the Order of Merciful Sisters, was arrested for kicking in the teeth of a truck driver who had shouted 'Hooray!' when Holland scored a second goal against Argentina in the World Cup.

### 2 BERT CLARK AND FRIENDS
In 1971–72, when Arsenal won the Double, Bert Clark, Ken Whiting and Ray Williams all fulfilled their promise to shave their heads.

'My wife won't talk to me,' Ray informed reporters.

### 3 KEN WOOD
In 1975, Ken Wood of Colchester emigrated to Australia after his team, Sheffield Wednesday, were relegated to the Third Division. 'I've torn up my rosette in disgust, burnt my scarf and given my rattle away,' he said. 'There's nothing to keep me here.'

### 4 HARRY BOSWELL
When newly-wed Harry Boswell named his home Goodison Park, painted it entirely in blue and wore blue pants on his wedding night, his wife divorced him, claiming that he loved Everton more than her. Six months later Harry married Tina Simmett. He wore a blue suit, socks and scarf to the ceremony, and straight afterwards rushed home to watch Everton on television. 'Tina understands,' he said.

### 5 PRESIDENT JIMMY CARTER
When the American ice hockey team beat the Russian team at the 1980 Lake Placid Winter Olympics, President Carter telephoned them in their dressing-room and said that between Iran, the economy and the ice hockey match, he had barely known which way to turn.

### 6 MR AND MRS KYLE
When George Kyle, a Newcastle United fan, married Gladys Taylor, an Everton fan, in January 1974, they left the church to an organ rendition of the 'Match of the Day' theme tune.

'So long as people have been properly prepared for marriage and take it seriously, I can see no objection to a tune like "Match of the Day" being played,' was the opinion of the vicar, The Reverend Brian Walsh.

### 7 JOHN ROBINSON

Though at thirty-five and a half stone he is the second heaviest man in Britain, Mr John Robinson regularly turns up to see West Ham play. But in 1975, he got stuck for some time in the West Ham turnstiles.

'I usually go to the games in my platform heel shoes, which leaves ample room for my stomach to clear the turnstile,' he explained. 'But I kept my working boots on and I got stuck. It took four blokes to pull me through.'

### 8 SIR FRANCIS DRAKE

On 19 July 1588, Sir Francis Drake refused to leave his game of bowls at Plymouth Hoe, even though the Spanish Armada had been sighted. 'There is plenty of time to finish this game and to thrash the Spaniards too,' he said. And he was proved right.

### 9 GODFREY BOLSOVER

Godfrey Bolsover wrote 25,000 letters in thirteen months, spending £700 on stamps, until he had enough material to write a book weighing three pounds entitled *Who's Who – An Encyclopaedia of Bowls*, which was eventually published in 1959. Mr Bolsover described himself as only an average bowler.

### 10 EUNICE BENNETT

On moving from Highbury in London to Skipton in Yorkshire in 1970, Mrs Eunice Bennett, an Arsenal supporter, became so homesick for her team that she renamed her new home 'Gunnersbury'. But this did not allay her yearnings. For the first two seasons she commuted every fortnight to watch Arsenal's home games. In the third season this system was becoming too expensive, so she left her husband, Bob, an airline representative, to live with her mother near the Arsenal ground.

### 11 ABDUL BUKHATIR

The billionaire cricket backer Abdul Bukhatir is so keen on cricket that he occasionally flies to London and stays at the Dorchester simply to watch cricket on television.

### 12 DOROTHY PAGET

The eccentric racehorse owner Dorothy Paget once failed to arrive at a race meeting when her car broke down. From then on, her second chauffeur followed her in a spare car whenever she went to the races.

## 13 DUNCAN PERRET AND FRIENDS

Glasgow Rangers fan Duncan Perret and three of his friends smuggled themselves in and out of Russia to watch Rangers play in Kiev. 'We got a train from London to Paris and then we hitched lifts to the Soviet border,' he explained. 'We waited till dark and then we sneaked over. The four of us then walked a hundred miles until we eventually got a lift to Kiev. Nothing could have stopped us watching that match, not even the threat of Siberia.' On his return, he was made secretary of the Supporters' Association.

## 14 THE AUSTRALIAN PUBLIC

In 1970, *The Australian* newspaper listed the names of twenty-six well-known Australians and polled people to identify them. 96% recognized Jack Brabham, 85% the Australian athlete Ron Clarke, and only 16% Patrick White, Australia's best known author.

## 15 THE AMERICAN PUBLIC

On 8 May 1970, at a time when American troops had invaded Cambodia and four anti-war demonstrators had been shot dead at Kent State University by the National Guard, President Nixon changed his regular time for addressing the nation from 9 p.m. to 10 p.m. to avoid interfering with the broadcasting of the final game between the New York Knickerbockers and the Los Angeles Lakers basketball teams.

## The **Fears** of 7 Sportsmen

## 1 BEING STARED AT

In February 1981, Gillian Gilks had an operation on her nose costing £700. 'I'm still not naturally gregarious,' she commented later, 'but I feel more self-confident. I don't walk along the street now and think everyone is staring at me because of my nose.'

## 2 BECOMING AN UMPIRE

In 1977, John Snow told a High Court during the Packer hearings that he suffered nightmares about having to become an umpire when he retired as a cricketer.

## 3 VIRGINIA WADE'S SERVICE

Chris Lloyd has admitted that during the first two games she ever played against Virgina Wade she had to fight the urge to duck whenever Wade served.

### 4 GOING BALD
English bullfighter Henry Higgins had a recurring nightmare about going bald. The dream took place in a bull-ring in Madrid. The bull was large and ferocious and the crowd incredibly enthusiastic. Then someone would shout, 'Baldy!'

### 5 HORSES
Barry Sheene is frightened of riding horses. He considers it too dangerous.

### 6 DISGRACE
In 1972, when Keith Murdoch, the All-Blacks prop, was sent home in disgrace after a scuffle with a security guard in a Cardiff hotel, he worked in Australia in anonymity for some months, so frightened was he of facing the music in New Zealand.

### 7 FLIES
Muhammad Ali hates flies and he hates doors being left open, thinking that they let flies into rooms. He also hates flying. Asked whether he was frightened of fighting Kolo Sabedon in 1961, he said, 'I'm not afraid to fight. I'm afraid of the flight.'

## 10 Key Words in **Field Sport** Slang and their Meanings

1 **A coney:** a rabbit

2 **A fag:** a small stag following an old one

3 **To serve:** to mate a horse with a stallion

4 **A good lepper:** a good jumping horse

5 **A charley:** a fox

6 **Cock over!:** the cry of beaters when a cock pheasant is flushed from hiding

7 **To paunch:** to gut a rabbit

8 **A wormburner:** a pigeon released from traps flying low at great speed

9 **Coffee housing:** talking at the covert side and disturbing the hounds

10 **Currant jelly:** the scent of a hare crossing the scent of a fox and disturbing the hounds

## 5 Sportsmen *Fined* for Strange Reasons

1 GLADSTONE SMALL IS FINED £50
In July 1981, Gladstone Small was fined £50 for wearing an advertisement on his bottom. Warwickshire manager David Brown had to run out with a pair of scissors and sticky plaster to patch it over. 'We positioned it on the backside so that it sticks out when the batsman is taking strike,' explained the advertiser.

2 PHILIPPINO BASKETBALL PLAYERS CAN BE FINED $133
In the Philippines, professional basketball players are liable for fines of $66.50–$133 if they spit at the referee.

3 JOCKEY WILSON IS FINED £1,000
In 1982, Jockey Wilson was fined £1,000 and banned for three months for bringing the game of darts into disrepute. This followed an incident in which Wilson had used abusive language towards an official in Dundee. 'This is going to cause a lot of trouble,' commented his wife Malvina.

4 SNOOKER PLAYERS CAN BE FINED £250
In October 1982, The World Professional Billiards and Snooker Association threatened to fine any member who failed to wear a bow tie throughout tournament matches the sum of £250. They also closed a loophole in the law whereby players could produce a doctor's certificate to excuse themselves on medical grounds. In future, only the Association's medical officer, Dr Denis Burges, can decide.

## 5 PETER OSGOOD IS FINED £100

In September 1979, when Peter Osgood refused to play in Peter Bonetti's testimonial, Chelsea manager Geoff Hurst fined him £100.

## 9 Notable Sporting **Firsts**

### 1 VIV ANDERSON

Viv Anderson was the first black footballer to play for England. He made his debut on 29 November 1978.

### 2 DOROTHY LAMBERT CHAMBERS

Dorothy Lambert Chambers was the first mother to win Wimbledon. There has only been one since then– Evonne Cawley.

### 3 DAWN FRASER

Dawn Fraser of Australia was the first and only swimmer to have won a Gold Medal at three successive Olympic Games. She won the 100 metres freestyle in 1956, 1960 and 1964.

### 4 PRINCESS ANNE

Princess Anne is the first and only woman not to be given a sex test at the Olympic Games since the introduction of the tests in 1968.

### 5 HENRY HIGGINS

Henry Higgins was the first and only Englishman to become a Matador de Toros, the highest accolade in bullfighting.

### 6 MISS R. D. TAPSCOTT

In 1929, Miss R.D. Tapscott of South Africa was the first woman to appear on the Centre Court of Wimbledon without stockings.

### 7 MARVIN HAGLER

In 1980, Marvin Hagler became the first boxer to appear naked on British television when he weighed in for his Wembley fight against Alan Minter.

### 8 THE GAYSTARS XI

In 1978, the homosexual soccer referee Norman Redman founded the first all-gay team, The Gaystars XI.

9  PETER WILLEY
Peter Willey was the first and only cricketer able to defeat Ian Botham at arm wrestling.

## The Top 10 **Football** Pop Songs

1 **'Back Home'**, sung by the England World Cup Squad. Reached number 1 in April 1970.

2 **'Blue is the Colour'**, sung by Chelsea Football Club. Reached number 5 in February 1972.

2 **'Ossie's Dream (Spurs are On Their Way to Wembley)'**, sung by Tottenham Hotspur FA Cup Squad. Reached number 5 in May 1981.

4 **'Ally's Tartan Army'**, sung by Andy Cameron. Reached number 6 in March 1978.

5 **'Leeds United'**, sung by Leeds United Football Club. Reached number 10 in April 1972.

6 **'Glory, glory, Man United'**, sung by Manchester United football team. Reached number 13 in May 1983.

7 **'We Can Do It'**, sung by Liverpool Football Team. Reached number 15 in May 1977.

8 **'Good Old Arsenal'**, sung by the Arsenal Football Club Squad. Reached number 16 in May 1971.

9 **'Tottenham, Tottenham'**, sung by the Tottenham Hotspur FA Cup Squad. Reached number 18 in June 1982.

10 **'Easy, Easy'**, sung by the Scottish World Cup Squad. Reached number 20 in June 1974.

## 8 Sportsmen who have earned Fast **Fortunes**

### 1 IVAN LENDL
In one week in December 1982 Ivan Lendl earned £187,500, or £26,000 a day.

### 2 EL CORDOBES
In 1979 this Spanish bullfighter earned £100,000 for a bullfight in Benidorm which lasted one hour and fifty minutes.

### 3 SUGAR RAY LEONARD
Even though Sugar Ray Leonard lost to Roberto Duran in the 1980 World Welterweight championship, he took home $8,500,000.

### 4 ANY DERBY WINNER
A horse which wins the Derby is generally worth about £10,000,000 at stud.

### 5 EVEL KNIEVEL
For his three-minute-long unsuccessful attempt to cross Snake River Canyon in Idaho in a jet-propelled 'Skycycle', Evel Knievel earned $6,000,000.

### 6 JOHN SMITH
John Smith is an Englishman who is a specialist place kicker for the American Football team 'The New English Patriots'. His job entails about ten minutes' on-pitch work each season. His contract for the 1983 season guarantees him a minimum of $200,000 a year, or $20,000 a minute.

### 7 BRIAN CLOUGH
After only forty-four days as manager of Leeds in 1974, Brian Clough was given a vote of no confidence by his players. He then left for Nottingham Forest with a £93,000 golden handshake.

### 8 JIMMY CONNORS
On 26 April 1975, Jimmy Connors earned £217,400 for beating John Newcombe in a challenge match at Caesar's Palace, Las Vegas.

## 6 Sportsmen who have Refused **Fortunes**

### 1 JAMES HUNT
In 1981, James Hunt turned down an offer of £2,600,000 from Jack Brabham to make a comeback. 'I gave it serious thought, but there is no point in risking your neck for money you don't need,' he said.

### 2/3 JOHNNY MILLER AND JACK NICKLAUS
In 1975, Johnny Miller and Jack Nicklaus turned down an offer to play each other in a million-dollar, winner-takes-all golf match. It had been proposed by Caesar's Palace in Las Vegas.

### 4 JACKIE STEWART
In 1979, Jackie Stewart turned down offers in excess of £1,000,000 to race for one season.

### 5 SUGAR RAY LEONARD
In November 1982, Sugar Ray Leonard refused an offer of $15,000,000 to fight Marvin Hagler and instead chose to retire. A year before, the retina of his left eye had been damaged and he was reluctant to damage it further.

### 6 MUHAMMAD ALI
Ali turned down an offer of $500,000 to act the part of the first black Heavyweight Boxing Champion, Jack Johnson, in a film. Johnson had a predilection for white women. 'I ain't appearing on no screen with no white woman,' said Ali.

## The 5 Things **Clare Francis** Misses Most on a Long Sea Voyage

1 Fresh milk
2 Salads
3 Hot baths
4 Ice cream
5 A vast library

# G

## 5 Memorable *Gambles*

### 1 CAN DEREK RANDALL STAND STILL?
A group of Nottinghamshire cricketers once bet their team-mate Derek Randall a pint of bitter that he couldn't stand still for ten minutes. After thirty seconds he gave up, saying that he wasn't thirsty.

### 2 CAN SOCCER SUCCEED IN AMERICA?
In December 1981, Jimmy Hill admitted losing more than £600,000 investing in American soccer.

### 3 CAN STAN BOWLES STOP GAMBLING?
When Stan Bowles decided to give up gambling and joined Gamblers Anonymous, a friend bet him five pounds that he wouldn't last a week. Stan Bowles won the bet.

### 4 FOR HOW LONG WILL DAVID SHEPPARD PREACH?
On the 1962 MCC tour of Australia, Colin Cowdrey, John Woodcock and Brian Johnston all placed bets on the time David Sheppard would spend over his sermon in Sydney Cathedral. After one false stop, he came in at twenty-eight minutes. Colin Cowdrey won.

### 5 CAN VITAS DRINK VODKA?
Ilie Nastase once bet Vitas Gerulaitis, a non-drinker, that he could not drink a giant tumbler of vodka. Nastase promised to take down his trousers and pants if he lost the bet. Gerulaitis succeeded in drinking the vodka, and Nastase had to perform his act to background music of Gerulaitis's somewhat tipsy yells of triumph.

## *Josh Gifford's* 5 *Tips to Young Trainers*

1 Realize that you are on call twenty-four hours per day.

2 Hard work and attention to detail.

3 Races are won and lost in the sales ring.

4 Always be tactful with your owners.

5 Do not gamble.

## 5 *Gimmicks* Employed by American Sportsmen

1 A PLUSH SADDLE
The female American jockey Robyn Smith sometimes used to ride on a saddle covered in mink.

2 FREE NYLONS
In a bid to attract larger crowds, The California Angels once presented every mother with a pair of nylons on Mother's Day.

3 A BLIND DATE NIGHT
In 1969, the Philadelphia 76ers staged an unsuccessful Blind Date Night, on which sixty fans paid to sit in a special singles dating arena to watch a match. Alas, of the sixty who paid, only four were girls.

4 A CHUMMY AUTOGRAPH
In November 1973, golfer John Miller's agent, Ed Barner, explained that he had insisted that his client should sign his autographs 'Johnny'. 'It has a more familiar, friendlier ring. John is kind of cold, not as affectionate as Johnny,' he said. 'But he prefers John, so when he signs his name he separates the "ny" from the rest.'

5 EVERYTHING BAR THE KITCHEN SINK
In 1951, Bill Veeck, the owner of the St Louis Browns Baseball Team, tried to boost attendance by buying 6,000 bats off a bankrupt manufacturer and giving them away to fans. When this ploy succeeded, he began to offer more and more free gifts, including Cadillacs, 20,000 Princess Aloha orchids from Hawaii, stepladders, cupcakes, two dozen live lobsters and five tons of nuts and bolts. Other gimmicks employed by Veeck included midgets selling midget hot dogs and an exploding scoreboard from which a fireworks display erupted every time the home team scored, to the accompaniment of Handel's *Messiah*.

## 8 *Good Sports*

1 LARRY HOLMES
Having defeated Muhammad Ali in eight rounds in October 1980, his former sparring partner Larry Holmes said, 'At that stage I held a few punches back for fear of hurting him. He was a great man, a great athlete and he was my friend.'

2 JACK NICKLAUS
In the 1969 Ryder Cup, Jack Nicklaus gave Tony Jacklin a four-foot putt, allowing Great Britain and Ireland to draw 16–16 with the USA.

3 DAVID JOHNSTON
In April 1982, when the Barbarians were beating Penarth by 84 points to 16 in the first match of their annual Welsh tour, the Barbarians captain, David Johnston, asked the referee to blow the final whistle five minutes early. 'I decided during the second half that enough was enough,' he explained. 'It had got to the stage where we were scoring nearly every time we had the ball. There was no pleasure in that. It was getting embarrassing.'

4 RODNEY MARSH
In the 1977 Centenary Test in Melbourne, after Derek Randall had been given out, caught at the wicket, Australian wicket-keeper Rodney Marsh called him back. Marsh had decided that he hadn't caught the ball before it hit the ground.

5 EUGENIO MONTI
In the 1964 Winter Olympics at Innsbruck, Eugenio Monti, many times World Champion of the two-man bobsleigh, realizing his chances of winning the Gold Medal were minimal and noticing that Tony Nash's bobsleigh's bolt had broken, whipped out his own bolt and gave it to him. Nash went on to win the Gold Medal.

6 STEVE OVETT
Straight after losing the 3,000-metre race at Crystal Palace in July 1981, Steve Ovett was approached by Elizabeth, the five-year-old daughter of New Zealand athlete John Walker, and challenged to a running race. He immediately agreed. 'I lost that one too,' he later admitted.

## 7 KARL SCHAFFER

Having beaten the legendary Gillis Grafstrom of Sweden in the 1932 Winter Olympic Figure Skating Championship, Karl Schaffer of Austria said, 'Yes, I beat him, but he is still the world's greatest skater.'

## 8 JOHN LANDY

At the Vancouver Commonwealth Games in 1954, the only two men in the world who had run a mile in under four minutes, Roger Bannister and John Landy, were lined up to race each other. The day before, Landy trod on a photographer's bulb in his bare feet, causing four stitches in his left instep. Bannister beat him by a second. Questioned by the Press, Landy kept denying his injury, saying, 'You're dreaming, boys. There's absolutely nothing wrong with the foot. Bannister was simply the better man.'

## 5 *Grubby* Sportsmen

## 1 DICK ROSE

Dick Rose, who played in goal for Wales twenty-three times between 1899 and 1911, and for many years with Stoke and Sunderland, never once washed his shirt, believing that bad luck would come to him if he ever did. He was a qualified doctor.

## 2 W. G. GRACE

Viscount Cobham once said of W.G. Grace, 'He has one of the dirtiest necks I have ever kept wicket behind.'

## 3 EVEREST MOUNTAINEERS

In 1983, new rules were passed which stated that anyone who climbed up Everest was expected to clear up their own rubbish. This followed an excess of rubbish being deposited on the mountain by hundreds of climbers each year. Everest now has to be booked up a year in advance for a climb, so popular has it become.

## 4 POP STAR BOWLERS

After the first Canned Heat Bowling Tournament in 1973, in which five different pop groups competed, cheered on by celebrities like Dusty Springfield and Kris Kristofferson, the disenchanted manager of the Los Angeles alley reported that fifteen bowling balls had gone missing, and that all those which remained had had their holes filled with potato salad.

## 5 ESSEX COUNTY CRICKETERS
In 1980, when several Essex county cricketers had gone down with a flu virus, spin bowler Ray East walked up and down in front of the dressing-room with a placard marked 'Unclean'.

## 5 Sportsmen who have been Found *Guilty* in Court

### 1 VERE THOMAS GOOLD
Vere Thomas 'St Leger' Goold, beaten by Canon J.T. Hartley in the 1879 Wimbledon final, is the first and only Wimbledon finalist ever to be tried and convicted for murder.

### 2 JOHN CONTEH
In March 1981, John Conteh was fined £100 for throwing a waiter across two tables in Conteh's own restaurant. A year later he was acquitted of a charge of leaving a pub in South London without paying for two bottles of champagne and a steak sandwich, on the grounds that he was not in a fit state at the time. He had been planning to call his drinking companion as a witness, but could not remember who it was.

### 3 JACK JOHNSON
In 1913, the black boxer Jack Johnson was found guilty on several charges of immorality after a Mrs Cameron Falconet had claimed that he had abducted her daughter Lucille, whom he had married a year before. Johnson fled with his wife to Canada and then to Europe in order to escape imprisonment.

### 4 GEORGE BEST
In January 1973, Stefanja Sloniecka took George Best to court for slapping her at a Manchester night club. She had slapped him back, but still he was ordered to pay her £25.

### 5 JONAH BARRINGTON

When he was a student, Jonah Barrington stole a wheelbarrow in the Earl's Court Road. He was found guilty of petty larceny while under the influence of alcohol and fined £10.

## 5 *Sporting Events Marred by* **Gunshots**

### 1 A SICILIAN FOOTBALL MATCH

On 4 January 1974 at a football match in Syracuse, Sicily, a fan fired two shots from a double-barrelled hunting gun into the air and demanded that a player who had been sent off be sent back on. The referee bowed to his wishes. The fan gained an additional advantage from his action: the visiting team from the North of Italy was so shaken by the gunfire that they let an additional seven goals into their net.

### 2 A ZAMBIAN GOLF TOURNAMENT

In 1976, David Moore, a 22-year-old pro from Brentwood, Essex, was shot dead while competing in an Open Golf Tournament in Zambia. The man who shot him, his host, then shot himself.

### 3 A ROYAL SHOOT AT SIX MILE BOTTOM

During a shoot at Six Mile Bottom, King Edward VII mistook a beater for a hare, fired at him and shot off his kneecap. The King obligingly paid the beater regular compensation for the rest of his life.

### 4 A RIO PRETO FOOTBALL MATCH

At a match between the Corinthians and Rio Preto, Joachim Isadore let in the fastest goal in football history. It had reached the back of his net within one second of kick-off. Isadore had still been saying his prayers when it whizzed past his head. His brother then ran on to the field with a revolver and fired six shots into the ball.

### 5 AN INDOOR ATHLETICS CHAMPIONSHIP

At the exceedingly cramped American Athletics Union Indoor Championships of 1974, the noise of the starter's pistol for the men's relay so startled a pole vaulter that he slid down his pole and collapsed.

# H

## 5 *Handshakes* which *Didn't Take Place*

### 1 MARVIN HAGLER DOESN'T SHAKE ALAN MINTER'S HAND
At the weigh-in before their fight in 1980, Marvin Hagler refused to shake Alan Minter's hand. 'I do that sort of thing only after the fight – never before,' he explained.

### 2 IAN CHAPPELL DOESN'T SHAKE TONY GREIG'S HAND
After a long-running feud during the 1978 World Series Cricket season, Ian Chappell refused to shake Tony Greig's hand. They now work together as commentators on Australian television.

### 3 ADOLF HITLER DOESN'T SHAKE JESSE OWENS' HAND
At the 1936 Berlin Olympics, Adolf Hitler refused to shake hands with Jesse Owens, the negro sprinter who had won four Gold Medals, because his victories contradicted Hitler's theories of Arian superiority.

### 4 HERB ELLIOTT DOESN'T SHAKE HANDS WITH ANYONE
Herb Elliott, the Australian champion miler, refused to shake hands with any opponent before a race, nor would he wish them luck. He said it would be hypocritical.

### 5 ERIC BRISTOW DOESN'T SHAKE HANDS WITH STRANGERS
Eric Bristow will never shake hands with a stranger. This stems from a time he shook a stranger's hand – only to discover that it was full of glass.

## The 5 Ingredients in *Giant Haystacks'* Midday Meal

1 Two pounds of steak
2 A pound of cheese

3 Two loaves
4 Two pounds of potatoes
5 Ten pints of milk

## The 8 Sports Most Likely to Cause you a *Head Injury*

1 Horseback riding
2 Judo
3 Boxing
4 Rugby
5 Soccer
6 Cricket
7 Hockey
8 Gymnastics

(Compiled by John Gleave, a neuro-surgeon who spent twelve years studying sport)

## *14 Famous People with Hidden Sporting Talent*

1 WILLIAM WORDSWORTH
Wordsworth was a keen skater and often boasted that he could cut his name on the ice with his skates.

2 OLIVER CROMWELL
Oliver Cromwell showed considerable skill on the football pitch when he was a student at Sydney Sussex, Cambridge.

3 MIKE YARWOOD
As a youth, Mike Yarwood had trials with Stockport County and with Oldham Athletic.

4 BING CROSBY
Bing Crosby is one of only two players to have holed in one at the sixteenth hole at Cypress Point in California.

5  GENERAL PATTON
Patton was fifth in the Modern Pentathlon in the 1912 Olympics.

6  GOETHE
Goethe was a keen player of real tennis. So too were Erasmus, Cellini, Hobbes, Rousseau, Montaigne and Sir Thomas More.

7  LORD BYRON
Byron used to enjoy sparring with John 'Gentleman' Jackson, the Bareknuckle Champion, in the privacy of the poet's Bond Street apartments.

8  DR BENJAMIN SPOCK
Dr Spock was a member of the American Olympic rowing team in 1924.

9  SIR ARTHUR CONAN DOYLE
In 1900, Conan Doyle bowled W.G. Grace out. In 1908, he was an official at the London Olympics.

10  THE PILGRIM FATHERS
The Pilgrim Fathers passed their time as they sailed to America on the Mayflower in 1620 by playing darts.

11  SIR TERENCE RATTIGAN
Rattigan was an opening batsman for Harrow.

12  MARY QUEEN OF SCOTS
In 1576, one of Mary Queen of Scots' most vociferous complaints when she was being held in captivity was that her billiard table had been removed.

13  JOHNNY MATHIS
In 1955, Johnny Mathis was ranked equal 85th in the world at the high jump. His best jump was 6ft $5\frac{1}{2}$ins.

14  PRESIDENT CANAAN BANANA
In January 1983, President Canaan Banana of Zimbabwe fulfilled a lifelong ambition by passing exams to become a fully qualified football referee. He sometimes plays football for the presidential team, The State House Tornadoes.

## 20 *Hyperactive* Sportsmen

### 1 JOHN CURRY
John Curry won the World, Olympic and European Ice Skating titles, all in fifty days.

### 2 JESSE OWENS
In the space of one hour in 1935 Jesse Owens broke or equalled six world records. In the notorious Berlin Olympics the following year he won four Gold Medals – the 100 Metres, the 200 Metres, the Long Jump and the 4 × 100 Metres Relay, and with each one set a new Olympic record.

### 3 WILLIE CARSON
Between his wedding and his wedding reception, Willie Carson dashed off to ride a horse at Chester. He won.

### 4 DAVID BEDFORD
In February 1970, twenty minutes after winning the Southern Senior Cross Country Championship, David Bedford went on to win the Southern Junior Cross Country Championship.

### 5 STEVE HOLLAND
At the World Swimming Championships at Belgrade in 1973, Steve Holland, the fifteen-year-old Australian, swimming in the 1500 Metres freestyle, first broke the 800-metre record by 6.2 seconds and then broke the 1500-metre record by 14.8 seconds. Most people would have considered this quite enough, but Holland did not realize that he had completed the course and went on another 120 metres before coming to a halt.

### 6 IAN BOTHAM
In Sydney in 1979, after Bob Willis had left the field dehydrated, Botham was England's only pace bowler left. He bowled eighteen overs. That night, after all the others had gone to bed, he went to see the film *Midnight Express* for the second time – 'to watch the gruesome bits'.

### 7 OLYMPIC RUNNERS
At the 1932 Los Angeles Olympics an extra lap was accidentally

added to the 3,000 metres steeplechase, making the total distance 3,460 metres.

## 8 MARVIN HAGLER
So keen was Marvin Hagler to beat Alan Minter in 1980 that he told his manager Goody Petronelli before the fight, 'Don't stop the fight for anything, not even my life.'

## 9 BILLY CASPER
The American golfer Billy Casper has eleven children.

## 10 MARY QUEEN OF SCOTS
One of the charges against Mary Queen of Scots at her trial was that only a few days after the death of her husband Darnley she had been seen playing golf on the fields near Seton. She was beheaded on 8 February 1587.

## 11 WILLIE SHOEMAKER
In 1953 Willie Shoemaker rode in 1,683 races, winning 485.

## 12 PAAVO NURMI
In the Paris Olympics of 1924, Paavo Nurmi won a Gold Medal in the 1,500 Metres and seventy-five minutes later won a Gold Medal in the 5,000 Metres.

## 13 ERIC HEIDEN
In the 1980 Winter Olympics Eric Heiden won the 500 metres, 5,000 metres, 1,000 metres and 10,000 metres Gold Medals on Lake Placid. 'Heiden is to ice what Mark Spitz was to chlorinated water' was the way in which the *New York Times* chose to describe this achievement.

## 14/15 JIM KELLY AND JONATHAN SMITH
At Fiery Creek, Victoria, Australia in 1854, Jim Kelley and Jonathan Smith fought with bare knuckles under rules which allowed a round to last until one man was knocked off his feet. The first round went on for two hours and even the fifteenth lasted one hour. For five minutes in the sixteenth round, both just stood looking at one another. Finally, Jonathan Smith conceded after a fight lasting six and a quarter hours.

## 16 BJORN BORG
In the 1979 French tennis championships, Bjorn Borg snapped the strings of no less than sixty racquets in two weeks.

## 17 HENRY HIGGINS
Between 1965 and 1972, English bullfighter Henry Higgins killed 170 bulls.

## 18 SIR GARY SOBERS
On 31 August 1968, Sir Gary Sobers scored 36 runs in one over against Malcolm Nash of Glamorgan at Swansea.

## 19 ALAN EVANS
In January 1975, Alan Evans scored 330 with six darts – three treble twenties with one throw and then three bulls with the next. 'It was unbelievable,' he said, 'I'd had a few beers.'

## 20 JACK BROUGHTON (1704–1789)
The boxing champion of England, Jack Broughton, was defeated in 1750 by Jack Slack. His patron, the Duke of Northumberland, was furious, as he had wagered £10,000 on him. Blinded and with blood all over his face, Broughton said, 'I can't see my man, Your Highness. I am blind but not beat. Only place me before him and he shall not gain the day yet.'

## *11 Sportsmen who have been* **Hypnotized**

## 1 BOB WILLIS
In 1977, Bob Willis first started carrying two twenty-minute tapes made by hypnotist Arthur Jackson as he embarked on his four-month winter tour of Pakistan and New Zealand. He claims that they stop him worrying, help him sleep, improve his concentration and give him confidence. In the 1977 series, he took twenty-seven wickets, the most taken by a bowler on either side.

## 2 GARY WINRAM
In the 1956 Australian swimming championships, Gary Winram was hypnotized to believe that he was being chased by a shark. But he still came second.

## 3 CRYSTAL PALACE
In 1979, Terry Venables called in a hypnotist to help Crystal Palace into the First Division. It did the trick.

### 4 JOE ERSKINE
Before facing Henry Cooper in the 1959 fight for the British and Empire heavyweight titles, Joe Erskine was hypnotized by Dr Philip Magonet out of his fear of the sight of blood. 'I've got a good left hook,' commented Henry Cooper. 'They can't hypnotize that.'

### 5 SEVVY BALLESTEROS
Whenever he is confronted by a problem, Sevvy Ballesteros listens to hypnosis tapes in his hotel room before he plays. After three seconds he can convince himself that the problem has disappeared.

### 6 REX STRONG
In September 1979, 21-stone heavyweight wrestler Rex Strong complained to the controlling body of wrestling that The Unbeatable Kendo had hypnotized him during a wrestling match.

'Kendo kept staring at me with piercing red eyes. Then he grabbed me round the throat so that I couldn't avoid his stare,' he grumbled. 'We were face to face. I couldn't move. It was as though I was paralysed.' Kendo then floored him with a flying crucifix leap and a pin fall.

The Unbeatable Kendo claims to be in contest with the 300-year-old spirit of a Japanese Samurai warrior. He retorted, 'I had beaten Rex Strong on a physical level. I wanted to totally destroy him on a mental level too. There was nothing he could do. I pointed my finger at him and he was rooted to the spot. There's nothing in the rules to say you can't use hypnotism.'

### 7 ROBIN JACKMAN
Bob Willis's hypnotist, Arthur Jackson, also hypnotized Robin Jackman into giving up smoking.

### 8 JOHN BUCKINGHAM
Before riding Foinavon to victory in the 1967 Grand National, John Buckingham went to a hypnotist, thus managing to reduce his weight by twelve pounds.

### 9 SOUTHPORT FOOTBALL CLUB
After being hypnotized by Romark in November 1975, Southport lost 2-1 to Watford. 'I think one or two played better for it,' claimed Romark.

## 10  DAVID BEDFORD

David Bedford attempted a comeback in 1977 by undergoing hypnosis from stage hypnotist Edwin Heath.

## 11  HALIFAX FOOTBALL CLUB

In January 1980, George Kirby, manager of Halifax, employed the hypnotist Romark for two sessions in front of his team before their FA Cup third round match against Manchester City. They won 1-0. 'He's a tremendous psychologist and inspired the lads,' said Kirby.

# I

## 6 Sports that have been Declared *Illegal*

### 1 BOWLS
During the reign of King Henry VIII, the playing of bowls was banned. It was thought that this would encourage people to take up archery, and would thus strengthen the army.

### 2 WOMEN'S FOOTBALL
In 1921, the year in which British women were given the vote, the Football Association banned women's soccer. Women were not officially allowed back on to the pitch until 1970.

### 3 MEN'S FOOTBALL
In 1314, King Edward II prohibited football in London, 'as there is great noise in the city caused by hustling over large balls'.

King James I banned football from the court of his son Prince Henry, saying that it maimed people.

### 4 GOLF
In March 1457, the Scottish parliament 'decreted and ordained that ... golf be utterly cryit down and nocht usit'. It too was seen as a threat to archery.

### 5 BARE-KNUCKLE PRIZE FIGHTING
Bare-knuckle prize fighting is still an offence against the law in England.

### 6 BILLIARDS
The game of billiards was banned towards the end of the reign of King George II. A fine of £10 was imposed upon public houses that were discovered to have tables.

## 6 Sportsmen who Enjoy **Impersonating** Others

### 1 STEVE OVETT
Steve Ovett can impersonate David Coleman and Johnny Mathis.

### 2 GRAHAM GOOCH
Graham Gooch enjoys impersonating his England team-mates, notably Geoff Boycott and Bob Willis.

### 3/4 MIKE HENDRICK AND GEOFF MILLER
Mike Hendrick and Geoff Miller have a double act routine in which they impersonate 'Sam and Arthur', two Derbyshire miners drinking in their local pub.

### 5 DAVE SEXTON
Dave Sexton can impersonate Jimmy Cagney and Boris Karloff.

### 6 JOHN VIRGO
Top snooker player John Virgo is adept at impersonating his fellow professionals.

## 9 Sportsmen who had Room for **Improvement**

### 1 A. J. LEWIS, GOLFER
In a competition at Peacehaven in 1890, Mr A. J. Lewis took 156 putts on one green without holing.

### 2 HARVEY GARTLEY, BOXER
In the regional bantamweight heats of the 15th Annual Saginaw Golden Gloves contest held in Michigan in 1977, Harvey Gartley spent the first forty-seven seconds of the first round bobbing and weaving, avoiding his opponent Dennis Outlette. He then threw his first punch, missed and collapsed. The referee counted him out.

### 3 FRANK MUIR, CRICKETER
'I am to cricket what Dame Sybil Thorndike is to non-ferrous welding,' said Frank Muir at the John Player League dinner in 1972.

### 4  IAN BOTHAM, RACING DRIVER

In May 1982, Ian Botham crashed two £12,000 sports cars going at 100 mph, in the space of an hour, during a racing day for personalities at the Thruxton race circuit near Andover.

### 5  KING EDWARD VIII, GOLFER

A tradition of the Royal and Ancient Golf Club demands that a newly appointed Captain must celebrate his appointment with a public drive. Taking over the appointment, Edward VIII, then Prince of Wales, had eight thousand spectators looking on when he swung his club and barely hit the ball, which trickled backwards three yards.

### 6  DAVE DUNN, BOXER

Mr Dave Dunn became a professional boxer in 1973. He lost both his fights that year, and both his fights in 1974. He spent the next three years recovering his strength before making a comeback in 1977. He lost again. In 1978 he took part in three fights and lost them all. He made another comeback in 1980 and lost twice more. In January 1981, he won his first fight after seven years in professional boxing.

### 7  THE NEW YORK METS BASEBALL TEAM

In 1963, The New York Mets, a notoriously poor baseball team, played and lost in Mexico City. When their manager, Casey Stengel, was asked if the altitude had affected them, he replied, 'No, my players can lose at any altitude.'

### 8  ORDUSPOR, TURKISH FOOTBALL TEAM

The Turkish football team Orduspor awarded their goalkeeper a £50 bonus after he had let in four goals against Gaziantspor in October 1980. The club's chairman explained that they had been expecting to lose the game by an amount of goals well into double figures.

### 9  STOCKPORT UNITED FOOTBALL CLUB

From September 1976 to February 1978 Stockport United Football Club lost thirty-nine consecutive League and Cup games.

## 17 *Injuries* which Haven't Stopped Sportsmen from Carrying On with the Game

#### 1 AN EYE OUT
At Puerta de Santa Maria on 1 June 1857, the bullfighter Manuel Dominguez had his left eye gored by a bull. He straightaway pulled it out and threw it away before carrying on with the fight, earning himself the nickname 'Desperdicos', meaning 'Garbage'.

#### 2 A BROKEN ARM
In November 1982, Birmingham City goalkeeper Jim Blyth played for more than an hour in City's 2–1 win over Sunderland with his right arm broken in three places.

#### 3 A BROKEN LEG
At Market Rasen in March 1978, Jimmy Beaton rode Romany Light in the Newark Storage Juvenile Hurdle with his left leg broken above the ankle. He finished fifth.

#### 4 A JIPPY TUMMY
In January 1982, in a darts match in Streatham, Alan Evans lost to Eric Bristow. 'I was suffering from an embarrassing stomach bug,' explained Evans. 'I was never sure when I might have to make a hasty exit.'

#### 5 A DISLOCATED NECK AND STRAINED RIB CARTILAGES
In 1964, American Al Oerter won his third Olympic Gold Medal for the Discus with a dislocated neck and strained rib cartilages.

#### 6 VERRUCCAS
In 1976, when he won the Olympic, European and World Championships, John Curry skated with verruccas on the soles of his feet.

#### 7 AN ABSENT LEG
Though Joseph Krubel (1881–1961) had lost a leg in the First World War, he still managed to climb the Matterhorn, wearing an artificial leg of his own invention.

#### 8 A BLACK EYE
Playing at a championship in Waterville in 1977, Nick Faldo was hit

in the eye by a golf ball that had been hit by his amateur partner. He collapsed, got up, went round in 75, and only then allowed himself to be taken to hospital.

### 9 A BRUISED HEAD
In the Centenary Test Match in Melbourne in 1977, Derek Randall was hit on the side of his head by a ball from Dennis Lillee. He carried on playing, and said afterwards, 'If it had hit me anywhere else I think it would probably have killed me, but as it hit me on the side of the head it wasn't too bad.'

### 10 A DISLOCATED KNEE CAP
In a bare-knuckle boxing championship in 1863 between Mat Hardy and Alf McLaren near Lal Lal, Sydney, McLaren fought for four hours on one leg, having dislocated his knee cap. In the twenty-ninth round, Hardy split his lip halfway to his nostril. After nearly five hours, both men failed to come up for the eighty-second round.

### 11 AN EYE OUT
Tommy Armour lost his eye in the First World War, but still won the 1927 US Open Golf Championship.

### 12 A WITHERED ARM
Though Ed Furgol had shattered his left elbow, leaving his arm withered and crooked, he still won the 1954 US Open Golf Championship.

### 13 AN ABSENT ARM
In 1824, the last year in which professionals were allowed to row in Oxford college boats, the Brasenose college four included a professional waterman who had only one arm and rowed with a strap.

### 14 ANOTHER BROKEN ARM
In a game during England's notoriously acrimonious 1932 Rugby League tour of Australia, the play was so intense that Queensland forward Dan Dempsey broke his arm and had it set, only to return to the pitch after tearing off his bandages and throwing away his splint, saying, 'At least I can get in someone's way.' At the same Brisbane match, Eric Weissel continued playing with a broken ankle, and the big lock, Frank O'Connor, refused to remain on a stretcher as he was being carried off the field.

## 15 DEATH
In June 1923, at the Belmont Steeplechase meeting in America, a dead man won a race. As the crowd rushed forward to congratulate the 20-1 outsider, Frank Hayes on Sweet Kiss, they discovered that Hayes was dead.

## 16 FAMILIAL BENIGN ESSENTIAL TREMOR
In 1981, Bill Werbeniuk revealed that he was allowed to write off against tax nearly £2,000 a year which he spends on drink. He suffers from a condition known as Familial Benign Essential Tremor, which causes him to shake uncontrollably in moments of stress. His doctor had told him that he would have to drink in order to become a top class player. 'Snooker is my livelihood and I like a pint, so it is a way of combining business with pleasure,' he says. 'I drink lager because nothing else works as well.'

## 17 TESTY TESTICLES
In 1973, as lawyers were preparing to fight a court action in which keen golfer James Baer was suing a fellow golfer for causing him 'permanent disablement' after a golf ball had hit him in the testicles, his wife Lynn gave birth to quins in a New York hospital.

## 14 Unlikely People who have **Inspired** Sportsmen

### 1 A DOCTOR
Alan Pascoe originally took up sport after his doctor told him it would help his asthma.

### 2 A HEADMASTER
Ian Botham's headmaster told him that he would be 'nothing but a waster' all his life. 'I am driven by proving people wrong,' says Botham. 'His words were an incentive.'

### 3 A MOTHER
When Virgina Wade was aged nine, her mother told her to clear up a junk cupboard. There she found an old tennis racquet. She then started playing tennis against the wall of her father's vicarage in Durban, South Africa.

## 4-6 CAESAR, CHARLEMAGNE AND NAPOLEON

Arnold Shwarzenegger has written of himself as a young man: 'I'd always been impressed by stories of greatness and power. Caesar, Charlemagne and Napoleon were names I knew and remembered. I wanted to do something special, to be recognized as the best. I saw body-building as the vehicle that would take me to the top.'

## 7 A PRIZE-WINNING FATHER

When his father won a local table-tennis competition, the young Bjorn Borg persuaded him to choose a tennis racquet as his prize. Young Bjorn then began treating it as his own.

## 8 AN AUNT

Chris Bonnington first went climbing aged sixteen, inspired by a book of photographs of Scottish mountains which had been given to him by his aunt.

## 9 A POLICEMAN

Asked why she had been so determined to shine in a man's game, cricketer Rachel Heyhoe Flint once replied, 'My first cricket memory is of playing it in the street with my brother and his friends, and a policeman coming up and taking their names. I asked the policeman to take my name and was furious when he said, "Girls don't play cricket".'

## 10 A VICTIM'S MOTHER

Aged five, Steve Ovett smashed a milk bottle over the head of a playmate. 'I had to run like hell to get away from his mother,' he says.

## 11 A GROUP OF CHILDREN

When he was in hospital suffering from cancer, Bob Champion at one stage gave up hope and asked a nurse to disconnect him. The nurse told him to walk around for an hour to see how he really felt. He walked into the children's ward. 'I looked at all the pitiful kids there, and that brought me back again and made me determined to fight it,' he says. 'If you see those little fellows still chirpy and cheerful in desperate circumstances it makes you feel very humble.'

## 12 A BIG STRONG FATHER

Former World Water-skiing Champion Mike Hazelwood took up the sport when his father threatened to beat him up if he didn't. 'As I was eight at the time, and he's 6 ft 2 ins, I decided I might as well give it a try.'

### 13 'THE BULLY'

Visiting The Maypole pub in Barkingside, Essex, Bobby George, who had only played darts twice, asked a regular known as 'The Bully' for a game. The Bully said that he only played for money, and that as he had twelve years' experience it wouldn't be worth the effort. But George persevered: 'I said, "Okay, seeing as you're The Bully and you think you're Jack the Lad, give me a week to learn your stupid game and I'll come back and play you for a £10 stake".' George then practised every night for a week, returned to The Maypole and easily defeated The Bully.

### 14 BRAINWASHING NEIGHBOURS

Willie Carson originally wanted to be a footballer, but it soon became apparent to him that his size would be a hindrance. 'People kept saying, "Aren't you wee, you ought to be a jockey." I heard it so often that I was brainwashed, and eventually I said "All right, I'll try to be a jockey".'

## 20 Sporting *Insults*

### 1 'You have as much class as my backside.'
*Cliff Thorburn to Steve Davis (World Snooker Championship semi-final, 1981).*

### 2 'For a kid to assume he can train a horse "The Woodhouse Way" would be as dangerous as turning a motorcyclist loose and allowing him to go the wrong way up a motorway without a crash helmet.'
*Harvey Smith on Barbara Woodhouse.*

### 3 'If Everton were playing down at the bottom of my garden, I'd draw the curtains.'
*Bill Shankly on Everton.*

### 4 'You are lower than dirt.'
*John McEnroe to Bill Scanlon.*

5 '**Cry Baby.**'
*John Sadri to John McEnroe.*

6 '**He's not so much a coach as a hearse.**'
*Tommy Docherty on a coach.*

7 '**It is all very attractive, the talent, the tears, the tantrums, the highs and lows, and all that so-called human stuff, but underneath there is a selfishness and ruthlessness that makes me look like a choirboy.**'
*Steve Davis on Alex Higgins.*

8 '**When I question an umpire's decision. I do it with good humour. McEnroe gets too angry and he should be stopped.**'
*Ilie Nastase on John McEnroe.*

9 '**He floats like a butterfly and stings like one too.**'
*Brian Clough on Trevor Brooking.*

10 '**He has done as much for the image of our sport as Cyril Smith would do for hang-gliding.**'
*Reg Bowden on Eddie Waring.*

11 '**Novice is the kindest word for the way he ran. And it's not the word I used to him. He ran like a chump.**'
*Peter Coe on Sebastian Coe (after Coe had lost to Ovett in the Olympics).*

12 '**Get out of the way, Grandad.**'
*Lester Piggott to Sir Gordon Richards (shouted during a race).*

13 '**He's a clown and that's putting it mildly. He sounds like an idiot, always talking to himself.**'
*Graham Yallop on Derek Randall.*

14 '**I wish his dad had taken him to Sunday School instead of the pub all those years ago.**'
*Tony Brown on Eric Bristow.*

15 '**I never really liked Big Daddy. I have no time for him. He's not a man's man in my opinion. I don't think he's the nice guy others reckon he is.**'
*Giant Haystacks on Big Daddy.*

16 'There are persons who are born to be stupid.'
*Guillermo Vilas on John Sadri.*

17 'He can't run, he can't tackle and he can't head a ball. The only time he goes forward is to toss the coin.'
*Tommy Docherty on Ray Wilkins.*

18 'They are disgusting, horrible people who have no loyalty. If I could have one wish it would be that I had never been born to them.'
*Joe Bugner on his mother and sister (after his mother and sister had complained that he had become superior to them, 1983).*

19 Asked, 'Were you playing for the English team in the 1950 World Cup?' Alf Ramsey replied, 'Yes, I was the only one who was.'
*Alf Ramsey on his team-mates.*

20 'I don't like Wilson and he does not like me. For him to win the title in 1982 was the worst thing that could have happened to darts.'
*Eric Bristow on Jocky Wilson.*

## The *Insurance Rating* for 20 Dangerous Amateur Sports

7 × NORMAL RATES
Potholing

5 × NORMAL RATES
Parachuting
Motorized hang gliding
Winter sports
Boxing
Paragliding

4 × NORMAL RATES
Horseriding
Hunting
Scuba diving with air tanks
Polo

Rugby
Martial arts
Snow skiing
Private pilot

3 × NORMAL RATES
Motorbike scrambling
Stockcar driving
Waterskiing
Ice skating
Football

2 × NORMAL RATES
Cricket

(All figures approximate)

## 5 Games which have been Unexpectedly **Interrupted**

### 1 GOLF AT LEITH, 1641
While playing golf in 1641, King Charles I was much disconcerted to be brought news of the Irish Rebellion.

### 2 WRESTLING AT THE HALIFAX CIVIC HALL, 1975
While Big Daddy and Giant Haystacks were wrestling at the Halifax Civic Hall in 1975, Len Hodgkinson, a 5ft 1in fan of Big Daddy, leapt into the ring and started pulling Giant Haystacks' hair. 'I gave him a warding-off blow, not a punch,' said Giant Haystacks. But the warding-off blow knocked out Mr Hodgkinson. When Mr Hodgkinson came round, he explained his behaviour: 'Haystacks wasn't fighting a bit fair,' he said, 'and he got me mad.'

### 3 GOLF AT KINGARTH, 1970
In August 1970, a group of lady golfers enjoying a quiet game on the Kingarth links on the Isle of Bute were surprised to have their recreation interrupted by a torpedo whizzing over the rough and landing on the first green. An apologetic Navy later collected it.

### 4 BOXING IN CANADA, 1970
In 1970, in the middle of a fight between George Foreman and George Chuvalo, Mrs Chuvalo jumped into the ring and insisted that the fight must end. Her husband was losing at the time. The referee brought the fight to a halt. 'He won't use his head. I've tried again and again to get him to quit,' said Mrs Chuvalo.

### 5 SOCCER IN AMERICA, 1967
When TV soccer was first launched in America in 1967, spectators were bemused by the curious and unexplained stoppages by referees. Three weeks later, the reason was revealed: the television company which was sponsoring the games had insisted on a set number of advertising breaks. Referees had to keep electronic devices strapped to their backs. 'I get three beeps on the radar thing and then I hear the producer saying, "A commercial coming up", so I have to get the play stopped,' explained the referee.

Following considerable outcry, referees were instead told to wave red flags at suitable moments such as penalties and offsides, thus paving the way for more logical breaks.

## 5 People who *Invented* Sports or Sporting Actions

1 **James Cribb of Croydon** invented table-tennis.

2 **James Naismith** invented basketball. Late in his life, he told a friend who had been appointed basketball coach at an American university, 'You don't coach basketball, you just play it.'

3 **Professor Jigoro Kano** invented judo. In 1882 he established the Kodokan Institute in Tokyo, still the world headquarters of judo.

4 **A farmer called Lambert** invented the offbreak at Hambledon, Hampshire in the eighteenth century. A simple man, he kept bowling straight until corrected by the club's president, Richard Nyren.

5 **John Willes' sister** invented the overarm bowl. John Willes was a Victorian cricketer who used to practise in the nets, bowled to by his sister. Her large fashionable skirts made it difficult for her to bowl underarm, so she tried bowling overarm. Finding it very difficult to bat against, Willes tried it out on others.

## 9 Peculiar *Items Worn* by Sportsmen

### 1 THERMAL UNDERWEAR
Yorkshire wicket-keeper David Bairstow turned out for a New Year match in Bradford in 1982, to mark the start of his benefit year, dressed only in thermal underwear.

### 2 A WHITE HEADBAND
Bill Beaumont would always wear a white headband while playing rugger. 'It's to cover up my bloody ears, you see, to stop them getting more cauliflowered than they already are. They're hardly my best feature,' he explained.

### 3 A RUDE NOSE
In 1976, John Francome went up to receive his National Hunt Championship Award at a special dinner wearing a nose which looked obviously phallic.

#### 4 A SUIT OF ARMOUR
In 1912, the vocalist Harry Dearth played a golf match at Bushey Hall dressed up in a suit of heavy armour. He lost.

#### 5 A PIECE OF PLASTER
Lee Trevino always wears a piece of plaster on his right forearm when he is participating in televised matches. It covers up a tattoo saying 'ANNE'. This refers to an ex-girlfriend of his, and he doesn't wish to upset his wife Claudia.

#### 6 A FEDORA
Malcolm Allison could always be seen wearing his Fedora until it was banned by the Football Association. They claimed that it 'incites crowd trouble'.

#### 7 ZULU DRESS
From 1879 to 1880, a team called the Sheffield Zulus played all their football matches realistically dressed and made up as Zulus.

#### 8 A CONSTANT CAP
Geoff Boycott always bowls with his cap on. 'It stops the hair falling in my eyes,' he explains.

#### 9 A SNAP OF THE WIFE
Sugar Ray Leonard always fought with a photograph of his wife taped to one of his socks.

*. . . and one Sportsman who can't Wear what he Wants*

'If I could wear a flashing light on my head I would. But the rules of darts say you can't wear headgear,' says Bobby George.

# J

1  **Jocky Wilson:** worked at the fish factory in Pottery Street, Kirkcaldy, where he worked on the fin-chopping machine.

2  **Ray Clemence:** worked as a deck-chair assistant in Skegness.

3  **Alex Higgins:** worked as an apprentice jockey, a barman and a tailor's cutter.

4  **Cliff Thorburn:** worked as a dishwasher on the shuttle boat to Seattle.

5  **Tony Jacklin:** was a steamfitter's apprentice in the Scunthorpe steelworks.

6  **Joe Frazier:** worked in an abbatoir.

7  **Chris Bonnington:** a margarine salesman for Unilever.

8  **Henry Higgins:** a flamenco guitarist.

9  **Jeff Thomson:** a bank clerk, an engineering rep and a dock labourer.

10  **Joe Barbara:** packed Opal Fruits in Slough.

11  **Terry Griffiths:** an apprentice blacksmith, a bus conductor, a postman and an insurance agent.

12  **Graham Miles:** a fitter with Birmingham Corporation Transport.

13  **Bobby George:** a floorlayer.

# Jobs

14 **Lee Trevino:** a shoe-shine boy at a Texan golf club.

15 **Lawrie McMenemy:** a clerk in an education office.

16 **Barry Sheene:** a lorry driver.

17 **Maurice Hope:** a leather tanner.

18 **Eric Bristow:** a furniture salesman.

19 **Jayne Torvill:** an insurance clerk.

20 **Ray Floyd:** the manager of a topless all-girl band.


***Brian Johnston's*** *Selection for the Most Entertaining England XI*

1 Colin Milburn

2 Bob Barber

3 Wally Hammond

4 Dennis Compton

5 Ted Dexter

6 Derek Randall

7 Ian Botham

8 Freddie Titmus

9 Godfrey Evans

10 Johnny Wardle

11 Freddie Trueman

(Chosen from cricketers he has commentated on in Test Matches)

## 8 Items Used in Sporting Practical *Jokes*

### 1-3 A TOWEL, A MATCH AND A HOSE

Following a junior tournament in upstate New York in 1976, John McEnroe and fellow tennis player Peter Rennert lit a small towel and threw it into the girls' dormitory in the Concord Hotel. They then rushed in and sprayed the dormitory and girls with water. For this, they were expelled from the Port Washington Tennis Academy.

### 4-5 A UNIFORM AND HAT

Upon returning to Rumania, Ilie Nastase once dressed up as a passport controller and fooled Czech tennis player Jan Kodes into believing he could not enter the country.

### 6 A RUBBER SNAKE

In the US Open, Lee Trevino produced a yard-long rubber snake from the rough with the end of his driver, giving Jack Nicklaus a shock.

### 7 NATURAL ACTING TALENT

In August 1977, Don Shanks of Queen's Park Rangers pretended to be violently ill outside a hotel in Belgium. Stan Bowles, who was in on the jape, called an ambulance. When the ambulancemen came and found nothing wrong with Shanks, the Belgian police were not amused and locked the two footballers in gaol for five hours.

### 8 A GUN

Preparing for their big fight in the Phillipines in 1975, Muhammad Ali went with his entourage to Joe Frazier's hotel. Ali then hopped around the lawn imitating a monkey and yelling for Frazier to appear. When Frazier stepped on to the balcony Ali pointed a gun at him and pulled the trigger five times, shouting that he wanted to shoot a gorilla. The fun passed Frazier by. 'You don't point guns at people and play around with them. It shows just what kind of ape Ali is,' he said.

# L

## *Jim Laker's* 5 *Tips 50 Young Spin Bowlers*

1  Concentrate on spinning the ball correctly.

2  When you have achieved this, then master length and line.

3  Learn to bowl both over and round the wicket.

4  Don't be frightened of being hit. It happens to everybody.

5  Adapt your bowling to different types of wicket.

## *Last Words* of 6 Sportsmen

1  **'Oh God, here I go!'**
*Max Baer, heavyweight boxer, died 1959.*

2  **'Elstree.'**
*Graham Hill, as his plane crashed approaching Elstree, November 1975.*

3  **'Did we do it?'**
*Sir Henry Segrave, killed attempting to break the World Water Speed record, 1930.*

4  **'I can't feel anything in my right leg. I can't feel anything in my left leg. Doctor, are my eyes open? I can't see!'**
*Manolete, Spanish bullfighter, killed in a bullfight, 1947.*

5  **'Bury me twenty-two yards from Arthur, so I can send him down a ball now and then.'**
*Alfred Shaw, ex-England Cricket captain, died in 1907, four years after Arthur Shrewsbury, who had committed suicide. In fact the distance between their graves measured twenty-seven yards. When someone complained to the county committee, he was told that 'Alfred always took a five-yard run-up.'*

6 **'That was a great game of golf.'**
*Bing Crosby, who died after playing a round of golf in 1977.*

---

*How Much it would Cost you to Buy Advertising Space on* **Niki Lauda's** *Body per Season*

1 Chest: £180,000

2 Chin-piece: £45,000

3 Either side of eyes: £25,000

4 Arm decals: £25,000

5 On helmet above eyes: £45,000

*8* **Left-handed** *Tennis Players*

1 John McEnroe

2 Roscoe Tanner

3 Martina Navratilova

4 Jaroslav Drobny

5 Rod Laver

6 Guillermo Vilas

7 Jimmy Connors

8 Roger Taylor

## *4 Stages in **Ivan Lendl's** Understanding of the Tough World of Professional Tennis*

1 'McEnroe doesn't like Connors, or me for that matter . . .

2 '. . . And Connors doesn't like McEnroe . . .

3 '. . . And to tell you the truth McEnroe is not my favourite person . . .'

4 '. . . It is all very difficult.'

(*December 1982*)

## *7 Comments by Sportsmen on **Losing***

1 **'When I lose it's like a knife wound in the stomach. I hate losing.'**
*Jonah Barrington.*

2 **'Show me a good loser and I'll show you a loser.'**
*Paul Newman.*

3 **'If I drop a few games, so what? I never mind about losing. People are getting shot up and dying. In the great scheme of things, darts isn't really that important.'**
*Bobby George.*

4 **'I am absolutely delighted to have come second. Who cares about winning when you can be second? I love being runner-up.'**
*Tom Weiskopf to a reporter who asked 'Disappointed?' after he had lost the 1978 Kemper Open in Georgia by one stroke.*

5 **'Sometimes you wake up in the morning and wish your parents had never met.'**
*Bill Fitch, basketball coach, after a losing run.*

6 **'Nice guys finish last.'**
*Leo 'The Lip' Durocher, baseball player and manager.*

7 **'I feel like when the President got shot.'**
*Sonny Liston, on losing his title to Ali in 1965.*

## 7 Good things to say upon **Losing**

1 'I'm sick as a parrot.'

2 'I'm choked.'

3 'We threw it away.'

4 'You haven't seen the last of us by a long chalk.'

5 'I still say we're the better side.'

6 'It's the worst moment of my life.'

7 'I really felt we had done enough to win.'

## The **Lowest** Scoring Side in a Test Match – The Final Scorecard

NEW ZEALAND V. ENGLAND AT AUCKLAND, MARCH 1955

| New Zealand | 2nd innings |
|---|---|
| J. G. Leggatt | 1 |
| M.B. Poore | 0 |
| B. Sutcliffe | 11 |
| J. Reid | 1 |
| G.O. Rathbone | 7 |
| S.N. McGregor | 1 |
| H.B. Cave | 5 |
| A.R. MacGibbon | 0 |
| I.A. Colquhoun | 0 |
| A.M. Moir | 0 not out |
| J.A. Hayes | 0 |
| Extras | 0 |
| Total | 26 All out |

*(England won by an innings and 20 runs)*

# M

### *John McEnroe's* 5 *Favourite Rock Stars*

1 The Rolling Stones

2 Bruce Springsteen

3 Pink Floyd

4 Foreigner

5 Santana


### *3 On-court Tantrums of* **John McEnroe** *at Wimbledon*

1 **'I'm so disgusting you shouldn't watch. Everybody leave!'**
*To the crowd watching his first-round match with Gullikson in 1981.*

2 **'You're a disgrace to mankind.'**
*To Wing-Commander George Grimes, umpire in his 1981 semi-final against Rod Frawley. Having been given a conduct warning, he insisted that he had merely been talking to himself.*

3 **'You guys are the absolute pits of the world.'**
*To umpire Edward James in his 1981 match with Gullikson. McEnroe became further annoyed when James wrote down 'piss' rather than 'pits'. He said he did not like being accused of obscenity.*


### *4 Comments by* **John McEnroe** *on the Trouble he Causes*

1 **'So many times the crowd never understand what I am trying to say and just never give me a chance. I have a perfect**

right to point out to an umpire politely that he has made an error.'

2 'If I see something that's wrong I just have to say so. You could say I have a temper. I'm Irish you know.'

3 'People get very nervous when they officiate me. Anyone who doesn't think so is an absolute jerk. I'm partly to blame, but they're, like, jumping out of their pants half the time.'

4 'I wouldn't like to be an umpire for me, that's for sure.'

## Britain's *10 Most Popular Sports* **Magazines**

*Shoot!* (Football): Circulation 250,000

*En Route* (Camping and Caravanning): Circulation 240,000

*Ski Survey:* Circulation 208,000

*Motorcycle News:* Circulation 181,000

*Angling Times:* Circulation 123,000

*Motor Sport:* Circulation 100,000

*Match Weekly:* Circulation 95,000

*Angler's Mail:* Circulation 94,000

*Horse and Hound:* Circulation 91,000

*Camping and Caravanning:* Circulation 89,000

## **Dan Maskell's** *6 Tips to Young Tennis Players*

1 Watch the ball.

2 For groundstrokes try to contact the ball as near waist-height as possible – but only after the top of the bounce.

3 *Swing* the racket-head for groundstrokes.

4 *Punch* the racket-head through the ball when volleying.

5 *Throw* the racket-head when serving – never 'push' it.

6 Watch as many first-class players as possible in action – live or on television.

## 7 Memorable **Meetings** between Sportsmen and V.I.P.'s

### 1 DENNIS LILLEE MEETS THE QUEEN
On being presented to The Queen in Melbourne in 1977, Dennis Lillee asked her for her autograph. 'Not in front of all these people,' she replied. She later sent him an autographed photograph of their meeting.

### 2 BABE RUTH MEETS MARSHALL FOCH
When baseball star Babe Ruth was introduced to Marshall Foch, the Supreme Allied Commander in the First World War, he said, 'Hey, Gen, they tell me you were in the war?'

### 3 REX STERRY MEETS AN AFRICAN KING
When Rex Sterry was deputy to Herman David at Wimbledon, he had to entertain an African King. He asked him at the end of the day how he had enjoyed it. 'I have enjoyed myself very much here at Henley,' replied the King.

### 4 SANDY LYLE MEETS PRESIDENT KAUNDA
Sandy Lyle fell asleep while playing golf with President Kaunda of Zambia. There had been a sudden downpour and Lyle dozed off as they chatted under shelter.

### 5 MUHAMMAD ALI MEETS PRESIDENT MARCOS
After he had met President Marcos in 1975, Ali was introduced to Mrs Marcos. At his next meeting with the President, he said, 'I respect you more now. I have been looking at your wife. You are not a dumb man. You know how to pick.' Looking at Mrs Ali, the President replied, 'I can see you are not far behind.'

## 6 F. S. JACKSON MEETS LLOYD GEORGE

When Winston Churchill, who had been his fag at Harrow, introduced England Cricket captain F.S. Jackson to Lloyd George, Lloyd George said, 'I have been looking all my life for the man who gave Winston Churchill a hiding at school.'

## 7 HENRI DE BAILLET-LATOUR MEETS ADOLF HITLER

In the 1936 Berlin Olympics, Henri Baillet-Latour, the President of the International Olympic Committee, noticed that the Nazis had erected signs saying 'Dogs and Jews are not allowed' outside the Olympic lavatories. He demanded to see Hitler and told him that the signs were not in conformity with Olympic principles, to which Hitler replied, 'When you are invited to a friend's home, you don't tell him how to run it.' Baillet-Latour told Hitler that when the Olympic flag is raised over a stadium, the stadium ceases to be part of that country and instead becomes Olympia. The signs were removed.

## 9 Cricketers with **Middle Names** you can Poke Fun At

1 JEFFORD

Mark Nicholas, *Hampshire*

2 BILLSON

Nicholas Cook, *Leicestershire*

3 WENDELL

Wayne Daniel, *Middlesex*

4 ORLANDO

Roland Butcher, *Middlesex*

5 THEOPHILUS

Sylvester Clarke, *Surrey*

6 L'ESTRANGE

Peter Wilson, *Surrey*

7 TROUTBECK

John Barclay, *Sussex*

8 STIRLING

Garth Le Roux, *Sussex*

9 DYLAN

Bob Willis, *Warwickshire*
(*He added Dylan to his name in reverence to his hero Bob Dylan*).

## 7 *Miserly Sportsmen*

1 LESTER PIGGOTT
Once when he had been paid in cash for a large amount of money he
was owed, Piggott went into a dressing-room and asked a fellow jockey
to lend him some money. 'What about that lot you just collected?'
asked the jockey. 'I don't want to break into it,' replied Piggott.

He also used to boast that he had a system for beating the barrier
carpark system at Heathrow airport.

2 GINGER MCCAIN
In 1980, Red Rum's trainer Ginger McCain was fined £250 for
paying a stable girl below the statutory minimum wage. Stephanie
Summonite claimed that she had been paid only £40 a week by
McCain, £18 below the agreed minimum.

3 JOHANN CRUYFF
Straight after being awarded a £290,000 contract in 1973, Dutch
soccer star Johann Cruyff complained to reporters, 'Football doesn't
pay much.'

4 THE OLYMPIC COMMITTEE
An Olympic 'Gold' medal is in fact only made from silver gilt.

5 'THE DODGER'
When amateur jockey Stephen Stanhope crashed into a stray horse
and fractured his arm, seconds after winning the novice's race at
Newton Abbot in 1974, professional gambler Simon MacCartney

chased after his departing ambulance, wrenched open the doors and insisted that Stanhope be strapped into a chair and transported to the weighing-room, so worried was he about losing his money. On arrival at the weighing-room, they discovered that the stewards had allowed Stanhope to forgo a weigh-in.

6 JOHNNY MILLER
In the spring of 1975, millionaire golfer Johnny Miller withdrew his wife's credit cards because he thought she was overspending. The previous year he had earned $353,021 in prize money alone.

7 MARK SPITZ
Elected Sportsman of the Year 1972 by an American sports magazine, Mark Spitz kept one of the magazine's reporters waiting three weeks in Los Angeles, eventually declining to see him until a proper fee had been arranged. The reporter left Spitz's trophy in an outer office and left.

## 6 *Missiles* Thrown at Sportsmen

1 A BALLBEARING
In December 1982, Kevin Keegan was felled by a ballbearing which hit him on the temple during a Leeds v. Newcastle match. 'I never saw it coming, otherwise I might have scored with it,' he joked.

2 A COIN
In the same game, John Anderson of Newcastle was struck in the groin by a coin. 'I thought it was a bullet,' he said.

3 A CHANNEL SELECTOR
A television remote control channel selector was thrown at Sharon Davies by her boyfriend Neil Adams after she had admitted to him that she had agreed to give a pop star some swimming lessons. It missed her and smashed against the wall. She didn't turn up for the first lesson.

4 BANANA SKINS
While Bob Willis was giving an interview during the England tour of Australia in 1982–83, Ian Botham was lobbing banana skins at him

from a dressing-room window. Without turning his head, Willis said, 'He lives on them, you know.'

### 5 A DART

In 1979, Pat Jennings was struck in the arm by a dart thrown by a Nottingham Forest supporter. The offending supporter was gaoled for six months and banned from the City Ground for life.

### 6 A BEER MUG

Sitting with his girlfriend Mary Stavin in the Chequers pub in Duke Street, London, in January 1983, George Best had a beer mug smashed over his head. Sean Murphy, a 49-year-old steel erector, was later sent to prison for two months. 'The police said to us that he did it because George signed for Manchester United instead of Liverpool,' said Miss Stavin.

## 5 Embarrassing **Mistakes** Made by Sportsmen

### 1 THE MISTAKEN DRUG DOSE

Before the 1961 Derby, the ante-post favourite, Pinturischio, was so powerfully doped that he was far too ill to take part.

### 2 THE MISTAKEN REQUEST

Bobby George once had to share an hotel room with Jocky Wilson. 'He walks in with a toilet bag,' recounts George, 'and I say can I borrow his toothpaste? So he takes everything out of the bag and rummages through it. Then he screams at me, "What would I be needing toothpaste for?" Laugh? – We were creased.'

### 3 THE MISTAKEN CRICKET BAT

Playing for Somerset against Nottingham in 1930, C.C. Case was so surprised to be given out under the 'hit wicket' clause, that in his trance he left the pitch carrying one of the stumps, thinking it was his bat.

### 4 THE MISTAKEN ODDS

In 1981, Godfrey Evans, who is employed by Ladbrokes as a special adviser on cricket, advised them to give 500–1 odds against England beating Australia in the third Test. But England won. 'I am absolutely stumped,' said Evans. Ladbrokes promised that they would still retain his services.

## 5 THE MISTAKEN MARKING

On the last round of the US Masters Tournament in 1968, Roberto de Vicenzo sank a putt for a birdie three on the seventeenth hole in the last round. His partner accidentally marked him down for a four, only realizing his mistake when the card had been signed and tested. But the realization came too late, and de Vicenzo lost by one stroke to Bob Goalby.

## 5 **Modest Moments** in the Lives of the Most Humble Sportsmen

1 **'I am the shop front. He's the goods in the back.'**
*Brian Clough on Peter Taylor.*

2 **'Really, I'm very shy and quiet.'**
*John McEnroe, 1981.*

3 **'I'm just another nigger who's trying to get bigger.'**
*Muhammad Ali.*

4 **'I'm not a diplomat – I'm Tommy Docherty – you either take me or leave me.'**
*Tommy Docherty.*

5 **'I'm no gorilla. I'm a pretty quiet sort of bloke really.'**
*Jeff Thomson.*

## For a Few Dollars More – What Sportsmen have Done for **Money**

### 1 SELLING MANURE
Ginger McCain had a healthy trade selling Red Rum's manure for 80 pence a bag.

## 2 SELLING VOLVOS
Moscow Dynamo striker Anatoly Shepel was suspended, and labelled an unprincipled money-grabber, when it was discovered that he had been selling the Volvos that had been given to him by the Soviet government.

## 3 CHANGING NAMES
In 1980, Nicholas Akers, a Canadian athlete, changed his name by deed poll to Nicholas Vladivar in return for money from the vodka firm from Warrington. But when he did badly in the Commonwealth Games, Vladivar withdrew their contract. In October 1982, he said, 'Look, I'm anyone's if the price is right. I'm quite prepared to become Nicholas Colgate, Nicholas Rice Krispies, Nicholas Newcastle Brown or Nicholas Aspirin as long as someone comes up with the cash to keep me running.'

## 4 SELLING AUTOGRAPHS
Before fighting Sonny Liston in 1963, Cassius Clay was only prepared to sign autographs on payment of a dollar. This he would then donate to three young black musicians who were accompanying him. When one fan offered only 50 cents, Clay replied, 'Come on man, don't put no fifty cents in there, get that dollar bill out. Think of all you're getting free here – the music's so fine and here you got Cassius Clay in front of you in living colour, the next Heavyweight Champion of the World, the man who's gonna put old man Liston into orbit.'

## 5 PLAYING AT WIMBLEDON
In 1981, Vitas Gerulaitis said that he only ever played at Wimbledon because his clothing and racquet contracts stipulated that he had to.

## 6 SELLING BADGES
In 1972, the Soviet Press announced that some athletes had been found guilty of selling badges awarded to them for sporting excellence. A Master of Sport badge was fetching 35 roubles.

## 7 RENTING A STABLE
A trainer at a Lewes stables used to rent out a top floor room over-looking the Lewes prison gallows. He sold space to watch the murderer of the 'brides in the bath' at £5 a head.

## 5 Sportsmen who have Enjoyed their **Money**

### 1 MUHAMMAD ALI
At the height of his fame, Ali used to cash cheques at Washington's
Federal Reserve Building, the only bank with enough ready cash. 'I'll
do anything for publicity,' he once said. 'I'll bring a pretty girl to the
gym every day if it is going to get me another $50,000 in eating
money.'

### 2 TONY McGRAW
The American baseball star Tony McGraw said of his $75,000 salary
in 1976, '90% I'll spend on good times – women and Irish whiskey –
the other 10% I'll probably waste.'

### 3 FRED TRUEMAN
Commentating on television about the good attendance at the Melbourne Test in December 1982, Fred Trueman said, 'That means
money, and that's what cricket's all about.'

### 4 BABE RUTH
At the height of his legendary baseball career, Babe Ruth was asked
what he thought of being paid more money in a year than President
Hoover. 'I had a better year than he did,' he replied.

### 5 MAJOR HOLLIDAY'S TRAINERS
The successful owner-breeder Major Holliday used to say of his
trainers, 'They come to me on bicycles, but they all leave in Bentleys.'

## 4 Sportsmen who are Not Over-Fond of **Money**

### 1 TERRY GRIFFITHS
In 1982, Terry Griffiths said, 'Compared with the jobs I used to do,
this is money for old rope.'

### 2 JOHNNY MILLER
In 1974, Johnny Miller said, 'I have had a hard time trying to spend
my money. All my clothes are free and so is the golf equipment.'

However, his wife obviously didn't find it as hard: in 1975 he withdrew her allowance, complaining that she was spending too much.

### 3 MARK SPITZ
After winning his five Olympic Gold Medals in 1972, Mark Spitz said, 'For me winning a Gold Medal was as important as winning a million dollars, because the medal was all I had to aim for.'

### 4 TOM WEISKOPF
Tom Weiskopf has for some time felt uncomfortable with the amount of money he earns. 'Why should a guy make $100,000 in two weeks? I like money, I play the game to win, but if you took the top five money winners of the year and took $50,000 from each of them it wouldn't hurt.'

## 7 *Mothers'* Views on their Sporting Children

### 1 **Mrs Kay McEnroe on young John**
'He isn't Attila the Hun. I really think he gets a bum rap.'

### 2 **Mrs Marie Botham on young Ian**
'He's a big softy really – full of life and fun, very determined on the cricket pitch but gentle as they come. He was the only teenage boy I knew who would always stop and talk to babies and small children in the street.'

### 3 **Mrs Knowles on young Peter**
'I think you're stupid, lad. I give you a month – no more – and then you'll be crawling back to that club on your knees.' (After Peter had left Wolverhampton Wanderers FC to become a Jehovah's Witness in September 1969)

### 4 **Mrs Shirley Lillee on young Dennis**
'He's as meek as a kitten.'

### 5 **Mrs Austin on young Tracy**
'We are lucky that Tracy is naturally a level-headed girl. Some of the tantrums you see in tennis these days would simply be foreign to her nature.'

6 **Mrs Margrit Bugner on young Joe**
'I've disowned Joe. It seems the family and me are not good enough
for him now he is a celebrity again. He may think he is a big man but
the only thing big about him is his height. I don't want to see him. I
don't like him any more.' (February 1983)

7 **Mrs Iris Sheene on young Barry**
'He has had to work hard to get money. He has never gone silly with
it and always used it wisely.'

## 5 Sporting *Mottoes*

1 **'Pain Means Progress'**
*Arnold Schwarzenegger's motto.*

2 **'Too Sweet a Life Leads to Trouble. That's my motto'**
*Frank Bruno, British heavyweight boxer.*

3 **Citius, Altius, Fortius (Swifter, Higher, Stronger)**
*The motto of the Olympic Games, adopted in 1922 on the advice of Father
Didion, a Dominican monk.*

4 **All That Glitters Is Not Gould**
*The motto worn on T-shirts by American swimmers in the 1972 Olympics.
Australian Shane Gould had won three Gold Medals, all in record times.*

5 **Festinalente (Make Haste Slowly)**
*Lawrie McMenemy's motto.*

## *Buster Mottram's* 3 Most Dangerous Tennis Strokes in the World

1 JOHN MCENROE'S SERVICE

2 BILLIE JEAN KING'S VOLLEY

3 JIMMY CONNORS' BACKHAND RETURN

## The **Munich Air Disaster** – What the 9 Surviving Players are Doing Now

**Albert Scanlon:** lives in Manchester, was a docker, is now unemployed.

**Bobby Charlton:** runs a travel agency in Cheshire.

**Ken Morgans:** is a window and door salesman in the Swansea area.

**Johnny Berry:** is a warehouseman in Hampshire.

**Dennis Viollet:** coaches in the USA.

**Bill Foulkes:** is the manager of Lillestroem, Norway.

**Jackie Blanchflower:** unemployed.

**Ray Wood:** sells sports equipment in the United Arab Emirates.

**Harry Gregg:** coached at Swansea City until his departure in 1983.

## 11 **Musical** Sportsmen

1 MIKE BREARLEY

Mike Brearley liked to hum to relieve the tension when he batted. His favourite tune for humming was the cello passage from the opening of Beethoven's Razumovsky Quartet.

2 JEFF BOROVIAK

American tennis player Jeff Boroviak plays a flute to calm him down before matches.

3 JOE FRAZIER

In 1972, Joe Frazier and his pop group 'The Knockouts' made an unsuccessful tour of Britain and Europe. Before fighting him, Ali once said, 'If Joe Frazier don't be sharp, he'll be flat.'

4 BIG DADDY

In 1980, Big Daddy released a single of his theme tune, 'We Shall Not Be Moved'. It failed to get into the charts.

## 5 JOHN McENROE
In July 1982, John McEnroe received guitar lessons from David Bowie. By chance they were both staying in the same block in Belgravia, and Bowie became so exasperated by McEnroe's attempts to play 'Satisfaction' that he went to McEnroe's flat and promised to teach him the next day on condition that he stopped that night. In August 1982, McEnroe and Gerulaitis played guitar at a charity show in New York on the same stage as Joe Cocker, Carlos Santana and Meatloaf.

## 6 JACK CHARLTON
Jack Charlton once released a single of 'You'll Never Walk Alone'. It failed to get into the charts.

## 7 HENRY COOPER
In 1977, Henry Cooper released a record called 'Knock Me Down With a Feather'. It failed to get into the charts.

## 8 THE AUSTRALIAN WORLD SERIES CRICKET TEAM
'C'mon, Aussie, C'Mon', recorded by the Australian World Series cricket team, reached number 1 in the Sydney charts.

## 9 ERICA ROE
In December 1982, to commemorate her streak at Twickenham, Erica Roe released a record called 'Remember Then'. It failed to get into the charts.

## 10 DON BRADMAN
In 1930, Columbia Records contracted Don Bradman to make a record. They thought that he would be giving a talk on cricket, and were somewhat surprised when the recording he made was of his piano renditions of the popular dance numbers 'An Old Fashioned Locket' and 'Our Bungalow of Dreams'.

## 11 KEVIN KEEGAN
In June 1979, Kevin Keegan's version of 'Head Over Heels in Love' reached number 31 in the charts.

# N

3 Children who were **Named After** Sportsmen

**1 John Robert Philip Peter David Vincent Colin Michael Paul
Arthur Keith Theodore Neighbour**
Born to Mr and Mrs Neighbour of Appleton Road, Eltham, in 1973
and named after the twelve players of Charlton Athletic. Mrs Neighbour also invited each of the players to be a godfather.

**2 Maria Sullivan Corbett Fitzsimmons Jeffries Hart Hurns
Johnson Willard Dempsey Tunney Schmeling Sharkey Car-
nera Baer Braddock Louis Charles Walcott Marciano Patterson Johansson Liston Clay Frazier Foreman Brown**
Born to Mr and Mrs Brown of Wrottesley, Wolverhampton, in 1974
and named after the last 25 heaveyweight boxing champions.

**3 Jennifer Pele Jairzinho Rivelino Alberto Cesar Breitner
Cruyff Greaves Charlton Best Moore Ball Keegan Banks Gray
Francis Brooking Curtis Toshack Law George**
Born to Trevor and Lynette George in December 1982. But when Mr
George told his wife that he had registered their baby daughter with
the names of his twenty favourite football players, she walked out on
him. She subsequently managed to cancel the registration and rename
the child 'Jennifer Anne'. But Mr George was not amused. 'I'm more
angry about her changing the names than her leaving,' he said. 'She
can stay where she is if that's what she's going to do.'

## 6 Sportsmen who are **Named After Famous Characters**

1 BIG DADDY
Shirley Crabtree (the real name of Big Daddy) was named after his
mother's favourite novel, *Shirley*, by Charlotte Brontë. In 1976, he
changed his stage name from 'The Battling Guardsman' to 'Big
Daddy', a name he got from a Tennessee Williams character.

# NAMED AFTER FAMOUS CHARACTERS

### 2 SEBASTIAN COE
Sebastian Coe is named after Sebastian in *The Tempest*, and his sister is named Miranda. Their mother was an actress.

### 3 GLENN HODDLE
Glenn Hoddle was named after Glenn Miller. His mother had just seen *The Glenn Miller Story* on television.

### 4 SUGAR RAY LEONARD
Sugar Ray Leonard was named after the singer Ray Charles.

### THE QUEEN'S RACEHORSE
The Queen named one of her racehorses Charlton, after Bobby and Jackie Charlton.

### 6 EVERTON WEEKES
Everton Weekes, the West Indies batsman, was named after Everton Football Club. His father was one of their keenest supporters.

*... and one House*

Lester Piggott's house in Newmarket is called Florizel, after the sire of the first Derby winner.

## 8 Sportsmen whose **Names** will Live Forever

### 1 FOSBURY
The 'Fosbury Flop' was originated by Dick Fosbury in the 1968 Mexico Olympics.

### 2 DERBY
The 12th Earl of Derby founded the Derby as a race over a mile and a half for three-year-olds of both sexes in 1780. The race would have been called the Bunbury if Lord Derby's friend Sir Charles Bunbury had not lost the toss.

### 3 ST LEGER
In 1776, Colonel Anthony St Leger, considering most races too tough

on horses, founded the St Leger at Doncaster as a race for three-year-old colts over two miles.

## 4 HARVEY
Californian surfer Tom Harvey had a great liking for the Italian Screwdriver (orange juice, vodka and galliano). After a day of surfing, Harvey would rush to his favourite bar, and drink so many that he would invariably walk into a wall on the way home, hence Harvey Wallbanger.

## 5 GIMCRACK
The Gimcrack Stakes at York is named after the most famous eighteenth-century racehorse. Gimcrack won twenty-seven races in all, though none of them were at York.

## 6 BECHER
Becher's Brook on the Grand National course is named after Captain Becher, who rode Conrad there in 1839. On falling into the water beyond the fence, he is alleged to have exclaimed, 'Water without brandy tastes even worse than I'd imagined!'

## 7 LEOTARD
Jean Leotard, who gave his name to the garment, was a nineteenth-century French gymnast, also famous for inventing the trapeze.

## 8 BOSIE
Though the Australians invented the term 'googly', they now call it a 'bosie', after its originator, B.J. Bosanquet.

## **Nothing New** – 5 Early Examples of Contemporary Scandals

## 1 DRUGS IN SPORT
In 3 BC, athletes were warned about using sesame seeds as stimulants. Chariot drivers fed their horses a mixture called Hydromel to make them run faster, and gladiators were doped to give them the courage necessary to make their fights sufficiently bloodthirsty.

## 2 THROWING MATCHES

In the Reverend James Pycroft's *History of Cricket*, published in 1851, there is a chapter entitled 'A Dark Chapter', relating incidents involving both teams trying to lose, each having bet on the other.

## 3 SOCCER VIOLENCE

In the nineteenth century, at Donnybrook Fair near Workington, four to five hundred colliers and sailors would play football all over the town. A correspondent to the local paper wrote, 'Fences are torn down; walls are scaled; and the game waxes fast and furious in the backyards of offending and peaceable citizens.'

## 4 CROWD DISASTERS

In the reign of Antonionus Pius (AD 138–161) the upper wooden tiers in the Circus Maximus in Rome collapsed during a gladiatorial combat, killing 1,112 spectators.

## 5 NOBBLING

One of the earliest recorded cases of nobbling was in 1778, when Miss Nightingale, owned by Hugh Bethell of Hull, was engaged to run at Boroughbridge. She was the clear favourite until the Sunday before the meeting, when she was found dead in her box. A post mortem revealed that she had two pounds of duck-shot in her intestines. A man was arrested and stood trial but was acquitted through lack of evidence.

# O

*7 Sportsmen who have had **Objections** to umpires*

1  GEOFF BOYCOTT
'You're a f . . . . . g cheat!' said Geoff Boycott to umpire Don Wesler in the 1978 MCC v. Western Australia match at Perth. Wesler had turned down an LBW appeal from Botham. When the umpire asked Boycott to repeat what he said, Boycott promptly did so.

2  ILIE NASTASE
'Come down off your chair and I will kill you with a ball in the mouth,' said Nastase to umpire Jeremy Shales at Bournemouth in April 1982.

3  JOHN SNOW
In his autobiography, *Cricket Rebel*, John Snow wrote, 'I can safely say that I have never come across another umpire so full of his own importance, so stubborn, lacking in humour, unreasonable . . . as Lou Rowan.'

4  W. G. GRACE
Once, when W.G. Grace was given out, he turned to the umpire, and said, 'They haven't come to see you umpiring, they've come to see me batting.'

5  R. P. NEHRA
In 1983, R.P. Nehra, the former president of India's cricket board, claimed that his side, trailing 2-0 in the Test series against Pakistan, were having to defeat eleven players and two Pakistani umpires.

6  GUILLERMO VILAS
At the Australian Open Tennis Championships in December 1981, Guillermo Vilas was warned by the umpire for exceeding the ninety seconds allowed to change ends. 'Do they think they're Almighty God?' complained Vilas. 'I think they should be a little quiet and know when to apply the rule.'

7  IAN BOTHAM

In January 1983, Ian Botham complained about the standard of umpiring on England's tour of Australia. 'You felt we had to get fourteen of their wickets and they only had to get ten of ours,' he said. After this remark had been reported in the *Sun* newspaper, Botham was fined £200 by England tour manager Doug Insole.

## 8 Odd *Odds*

1  The odds against a flat race horse paying for its keep over a year are 10–1, and for a steeplechaser 20–1.

2  The odds for a steeplechase jockey ending a race unseated are also 10–1.

3  The odds for a Channel swimmer completing the swim successfully are 20–1.

4  The odds for a hole in one are 42952–1.

5  The shortest odds ever were 10,000–1 on for Lester Piggott to win the Premio Naviglio in Milan in 1967.

6  Talking to Michael Parkinson in 1974, Muhammad Ali reckoned that the odds of making a good living out of boxing were 'about 100,000 to one'. He advised potential boxers to 'get their brains together and get educated'.

7  In 1963, bookies offered odds of 66–1 against The Duke of Albuquerque finising the Grand National on horseback. He fell at the fourth fence.

8  In 1982, Ladbrokes refused any further bets on Liverpool winning the League Championship, even though there were five months of the programme still to be completed. Sure enough, Liverpool won.

## 7 *Officials* who were Not Quite Up to Scratch

### 1 THE SLEEPY LINESWOMAN
At the end of a match on no. 3 court at Wimbledon in 1964, Mrs Dorothy Cavis Brown, a lineswoman, was found asleep. 'I have had a very exhausting time lately,' she explained.

### 2 THE COLOUR BLIND REFEREE
In January 1981, former top soccer referee Keith Butcher confessed that he was colour blind. 'I couldn't tell the difference between the red and yellow cards,' he said. He once gave Everton a penalty when it should have been a free kick to West Bromwich Albion, and in another game he was unaware that both teams were wearing the same colour until a linesman spoke up.

### 3 THE PARANOID REFEREE
In December 1982, referee Peter Richmond sent off all thirty players in a Rugby match between Abingdon and Didcot in December 1982. This entailed their suspension for thirty days. Abingdon president Dave Morgan Scott protested, 'I would say the referee lost control. It is grossly unfair that innocent players should be suspended.'

### 4 THE DODGY STEWARD
It was rumoured that a steward at Windsor, Captain 'Wiggie' Weyland, once delayed the hearing of an objection because he was with his bookmakers, betting on the outcome.

### 5 THE POACHER TURNED GAMEKEEPER
After Derek Randall umpired a Nottinghamshire match in 1977 he admitted that he had nearly had a riot on his hands. 'I kept making the wrong decisions,' he said, 'so they chucked me off and made me run the line.'

### 6 THE INACCURATE UMPIRE
In the 1877 Oxford and Cambridge Boat Race, the umpire, 'Honest' John Phelps, gave the verdict as 'Dead heat to Oxford by six foot'.

### 7 THE OVER-PUNCTUAL REFEREE
In the 1930 World Cup Final in Uruguay, the referee blew his whistle six minutes too early. The teams then had to be brought back from their dressing-rooms in order to finish the game.

## *10 Sporting* **Old Timers**

### 1 SIR STANLEY MATTHEWS
Sir Stanley Matthews was still playing first-class football aged 50.

### 2 MRS ETHEL HEPBURN
In 1955, Mrs Ethel Hepburn of Pretoria won the Transvaal Croquet Championship aged 78.

### 3 JOHN THORNE
In 1981, John Thorne, a grandfather aged 54, came second in the Grand National on Spartan Missile.

### 4 DICK SAUNDERS
In 1982, Dick Saunders, aged 48, won the Grand National on Grittar.

### 5 PIERRE ETCHBASTER
Pierre Etchbaster held the title of World Tennis Champion for twenty-seven years until he retired in 1928 aged 60.

### 6 REG HARRIS
Twenty years after winning his fifth world title and seventeen years after his retirement, sprint cyclist Reg Harris, aged 54, won the British Pro Championship, in 1974.

### 7 MIRUTS YIFTER
In the Moscow Olympics, Miruts Yifter won the 5,000 and 10,000 metres aged between 35 and 39. It is impossible to say his exact age because he will not reveal it. 'I no count the years,' he says. 'Men may steal my chickens, men may steal my sheep. But no man can steal my age.'

### 8 A BARNSLEY FAN
In 1978, a 68-year-old Barnsley supporter became the oldest football hooligan in the world when he was fined £25 for spitting at a referee. 'I will try to control myself in future,' he said.

### 9 HASHIM KHAN
Hashim Khan won his seventh Open Squash Championship aged 42.

10 SIR JACK HOBBS

Ninety-eight of Sir Jack Hobbs' 197 centuries in first-class cricket came after he had passed the age of 40.

## *11 of the Strangest **One-off** Sporting Events*

1 THE BLIND PLAYING THE BLIND

In 1967, there was a forty-minute football match in Lima, Peru, between two teams composed entirely of blind people. They drew 2–2. The match was refereed by Sister Soledad Vasquez.

2 UNDERWATER DRAUGHTS

On 27 July 1962, naval frogmen attached to the Royal Naval College, Dartmouth, played underwater draughts while the Queen looked on.

3 HIGH ALTITUDE TIDDLEYWINKS

In 1961, on a tour of Africa, 'The Twinkers', Britain's tiddleywinks champions, defeated a team of Commonwealth players on the top of Mount Kilimanjaro.

4 A GO SLOW RACE

In October 1950, a French motorist, M. Durand, was the winner of a 'Go Slow' race along Rue Lepie in Montmartre in Paris. He took ten hours, forty minutes and fifty-one seconds to cover 722 yards. During the race, timekeepers kept competitors under close observation to check that their wheels moved continuously. M. Durand's wheels took an average of three minutes to make a complete turn.

5 ARCHERS V. GOLFERS

In 1976, a team from the Bridport and West Dorset Golf Club took on the Beaminster Bowmen Archery Club in a match over a golf course. The archers received a penalty shot each time their arrows landed in the rough. They had to aim at a disc the size of a hole. The Beaminster Bowmen won $5\frac{1}{2}$ matches, the Bridport and West Dorset Golf Club $3\frac{1}{2}$.

6 KARATE V. BULLS

The former world karate champion, Masutatsu Oyama, once engaged .

in bare-handed combat with fifty-two bulls, dealing sudden death to three and cracking off the horns of forty-eight.

### 7 WALKING BACKWARDS
Between 1931 and 1932 Plennie L. Wingo walked backwards all the way from Santa Monica, California, to Istanbul in Turkey, a distance of eight thousand miles.

### 8 A GREAT BRITISH SUCCESS
When the 400 metre race in the 1908 London Olympics was declared void, the two American runners refused to take part in the re-run. This left the Briton, Lieutenant Wyndham Halswelle, to run the 400 metres all by himself, at the end of which he was declared the winner.

### 9 THE ENERGETIC MARKSMAN
In December 1906, Adolf Topperween, an American, fired a pistol at two and a half inch wooden cubes which were tossed into the air. He fired once every five seconds for eight hours a day on nine consecutive days. His final tally was 75,000 cubes hit and only 9 missed.

### 10 NAILS V. DARTS
In August 1957, a darts expert using six-inch nails beat a novice using regular darts in a competition held in Long Eaton, Derbyshire. The expert had finished before the novice had scored his double to start.

### 11 THE WATER SKIER AGAINST THE CAR FERRY
On 21 September 1969, Michael Walker, a 22-year-old Bournemouth lorry driver, set off on a single ski across the English channel at the same time as the Viking car ferry. He arrived in three and a half hours, beating the ferry.

## 6 Pairs of Classic *One-two's*

### 1 BRIAN CLOUGH AND DON REVIE
*Brian Clough*: 'The Football Association should have instantly relegated Don Revie's team after branding them as one of the dirtiest clubs in Britain.'
*Don Revie*: 'We all know that Brian Clough can walk on water. I think it is time he shut his mouth.'

## 2  GEOFF BOYCOTT AND TONY GREIG

*Geoff Boycott (on the World Series players)*: 'Disloyal traitors ... Have bat, will travel.'
*Tony Greig*: 'Geoff Boycott has the uncanny knack of being where fast bowlers aren't.'

## 3  STEVE DAVIS AND ALEX HIGGINS

*Steve Davis*: 'You know, a lot of people are using two-piece cues nowadays. Alex Higgins hasn't got one, mainly because it doesn't come with instructions.'
*Alex Higgins*: 'Steve? Steve who? Is he the video game player?'

## 4  BARONESS SUMMERSKILL AND HENRY COOPER

*Baroness Summerskill was a notorious anti-boxing campaigner. This exchange took place in a television discussion)*
*Baroness Summerskill*: 'Mr Cooper, have you looked in the mirror and seen the state of your nose?'
*Henry Cooper*: 'Well, Madam, have you looked in the mirror and seen the state of *your* nose lately? Boxing's my excuse. What's yours?'

## 5  TONY JACKLIN AND LEE TREVINO

*(As they were playing golf in 1972, Trevino was talking a lot)*
*Tony Jacklin*: 'I would rather not talk.'
*Lee Trevino*:' I don't care if you don't want to talk. Just listen.'

## 6  KEVIN KEEGAN AND GEORGE BEST

*Kevin Keegan (in Leeds High Court in October 1982)*: 'Best had given footballers a bad name and I saw it as my job to repair their reputation. It took a long time and a lot of hard work, but I like to think I helped.'
*George Best*: 'Keegan couldn't lace my boots as a player. He's been very, very lucky, an average player who came into a game when it was short of personalities.'

*How to Regard your* **Opponent** *– the Views of 5 Sportsmen*

1  **'You don't go into the ring hating the man – not really hating**

him. You just go in there thinking, "Well, if I don't do him, he'll do me".'
*Henry Cooper.*

2 'When I see a rival owner or trainer cheering home a winner I have one reaction – I say good luck to him.'
*Robert Sangster.*

3 'I really hate having to play friends, or someone who's been in a team with me. I can't concentrate at all. That's one of the reasons why I have never really been very close friends with any one of the girls.'
*Virginia Wade.*

4 'I don't like any opponent. Ever. Never have and specially not now. I don't like any man who wants to take what I worked so hard for, waited so long for and which means most to me – my title.'
*Marvin Hagler.*

5 'The name of the game is to kill the quarterback.'
*Joe Namath, pro football star.*

## The **Origins** of 7 Different Sports

1 HURDLING
In 1850, at the Exeter College point-to-point, a small group of people decided that as the hired horses had been so disappointing they should hurdle themselves. They invented a two-mile course with twenty-four jumps and a bookmaker.

2 BADMINTON
In 1860, the houseguests at Badminton, the home of the Duke of Beaufort, were confined to the house by rain. Borrowing shuttlecocks from the nursery, they devised a game that could be played in the Great Hall without any damage to the china.

### 3 HORSE-RACING

It is probable that the first racing in the world developed from Arabs betting on which of their thirsty horses would reach a pool of water first.

### 4 RUGBY

Legend has it that Rugby was started when William Webb Ellis, a pupil at Rugby School, picked up the ball while playing a football match and ran with it. A plaque at Rugby School says: 'This stone commemorates the exploit of William Webb Ellis, who, with a fine disregard for the rules of Football as played in his time, first took the ball in his arms and ran with it, thus originating the distinctive feature of the Rugby game, A.D. 1823.'

### 5 SQUASH

At the end of the nineteenth century there were too many boys at Harrow School who wished to play rackets, so a new game was devised for the juniors, with a larger and softer ball and a smaller and cheaper court. This became known as squash rackets.

### 6 WATER POLO

In 1876, members of the Bournemouth Rowing Club were throwing a medicine ball about when one of them accidentally threw it into the water. Other members jumped in after it and began playing with it, thus giving birth to water polo.

### 7 THE MODERN OLYMPIC MARATHON

The Olympic Marathon distance of twenty-six miles and 385 yards was established in the 1908 London Olympics. It is the distance between the lawns of Windsor Castle and the White City stadium. Previously the course had been run over exactly twenty-four miles.


## The *Origins* of 10 Sporting Words


### 1 A DUCK

If you are out for 0 in cricket, this numeral resembles a duck's egg, hence 'out for a duck'.

## 2 LOVE

A score of o in tennis was also held to resemble an egg, for which the
French is *l'œuf*, hence 'love'.

## 3 SCRUM

'Scrum' is a shortened form of 'skirmish'.

## 4 GOLF

The first golf-like game was played in Holland in the thirteenth
century. It was known as *Spel metten colve* ('Game played with a club').
It was then shortened to Colve, and then over the centuries changed
from Colf to Kolf to Golf.

## 5 TENNIS

Tennis comes from the French command *Tenez*, the call of a player to
warn his opponent he is about to serve.

## 6 SERVICE

The term 'service' was introduced in the first part of the sixteenth
century when King Henry VIII and his barons played real tennis. It
was considered beneath their dignity to play the first shot, so they
would call 'Service' and page with a ball would start the game.

## 7 BOWL

'Bowl' is derived from the French word *boule*. In English it used to be
pronounced to rhyme with 'howl', but the vowel was softened by the
Victorians who thought it sounded a little too close to 'bowel' for
comfort.

## 8 THE ASHES

In 1882, after the third Australian team ever to come to England beat
England at The Oval, *The Sporting Times* wrote an epitaph on the
death of English cricket, adding as a postscript: 'N.B. The body will be
cremated and the ashes taken to Australia.' The next winter, an
English team defeated Australia in two out of the three games. The
stumps were burned and the ashes presented to the English captain
by the Australian captain. The urn is still to be seen at Lord's.

## 9 THE CRAWL

The word 'crawl' was first applied to swimming in 1898 by George
Farmer, an Australian swimming coach. On seeing Alick Wicham

winning an under-ten swimming race in Sydney he said, 'Look at this kid crawling.'

### 10 FIFTEEN–FORTY
Tennis used to be scored on a clock dial, hence fifteen, thirty and forty-five, which was later shortened to forty.

## 5 Sportsmen who have Scored for the **Other Side**

### 1 PAT KRUSE
On 3 January 1977, Pat Kruse of Torquay United managed to head the ball into his own net just six seconds after the kick-off against Cambridge United.

### 2 BABE MANOLEK
Before a big fight in Pennsylvania in December 1939, Babe Manolek's trainer advised him to try and knock out his opponent the second the bell sounded for the start of the first round. Attempting to do this, Manolek charged towards his opponent, slipped up and knocked himself out without having struck or received a blow.

### 3 ROY RIEGLES
In the annual Los Angeles Rose Bowl Football Championship of 1929, Roy Riegles, the lineman with the University of California, ran the wrong way with the ball. The more the fans and his team-mates shouted at him, the more encouraged he became. Thus he scored two points for the other side, Georgia Tech, winning them the Championship.

### 4 G. WELLS
Playing for Sussex against Kent at Gravesend in 1866, G. Wells hit his wicket while the bowler was running up to bowl and was given out, making him one of the few cricketers to have been out from a ball that was never actually delivered.

### 5 ROB NEWMAN
Having scored two own goals at Mansfield in 1982, Bristol City defender Rob Newman left the pitch in tears. In the comfort of the dressing-room he discovered his wallet had been stolen.

## *Over the Top* – *8 Sporting Exaggerations*

1 'If Chamberlain had sent a couple of battalions of goal-keepers across the channel in the autumn of '39 the Second World War would not have lasted a fortnight.'
*Byron Butler and Ron Greenwood, 1979.*

2 'If he was at Cape Canaveral he'd take off before the rocket.'
*Sid Waddell on Eric Bristow.*

3 'Physically, his impact knocks you in the mud. He's John Wayne and Goliath, with blue eyes and curly hair like Samson.'
*Jean Rook on Bill Beaumont.*

4 'You reflect all the ideals of our society.'
*President Jimmy Carter to the USA ice hockey team, who had just beaten the USSR team at Lake Placid in 1980.*

5 'Pro football is like nuclear warfare. There are no winners, only survivors.'
*Frank Gifford in 'Sports Illustrated', 1960.*

6 'Cruyff was manufactured on earth. Georgie Best was made in heaven.'
*Derek Dougan.*

7 'Brown tackles his opponents the way Desperate Dan used to tackle cow pie.'
*Sid Waddell on Tony Brown, darts player.*

8 'When two of us were evenly matched, it was a fusion of spirits. It was almost a sexual feeling. I felt we were entwined body and soul.'
*John Conteh on boxing.*

## STEVE OVETT

### *Steve Ovett's* 6 Hobbies

1 Practical sculpture

2 Cars

3 Reading

4 Angling

5 Painting

6 Photography

# P

*The 10 Most Popular **Participatory Sports** in England and Wales*

1 **Walking** (2 miles): 8.3 million

2 **Indoor Swimming:** 3.0 million

3 **Darts:** 2.9 million

4 **Billiards/Snooker:** 2.8 million

5 **Outdoor Swimming** (excluding public pools): 2.3 million

6= **Angling:** 1.2 million

   **Golf:** 1.2 million

8= **Football:** 1.1 million

   **Tennis:** 1.1 million

10 **Table Tennis:** 0.9 million

(*Based on a Sports Council survey conducted in 1980*)

## 3 *Patron Saints* of Darts

1 BRIAN GAMLIN

Gamlin, a 44-year-old carpenter from Bury in Lancashire, devised the present numbering on darts boards. He died in 1903, before he had had a chance to patent his idea.

2 JOHN READER

Reader, an undertaker's assistant from Sussex, attained the first recorded maximum score of 180 in a Sussex pub in 1902.

3 FOOT ANAKIN

Anakin was a Leeds publican who was prosecuted for allowing the game of darts on his premises. At that time darts was banned from public houses as it was considered to be a game of chance and not of skill. On trial in the Leeds magistrates court, Anakin obtained permission to have a dartboard set up. A court official was deputed to challenge him to a short game of three darts. Anakin threw three twenties. The court official only managed to get one dart anywhere on the board. Anakin then repeated his three twenties, and the case was dismissed. And so darts became an integral part of British pub life.

## 6 Peculiar **Penalties** Placed on Sportsmen

### 1 DEATH
In the nineteenth century, Lord Glasgow shot all his racehorses which did not come up to standard.

### 2 DISCRIMINATION
At the Montreal Olympic Games in 1976, women were allowed to spend the night in the men's apartments, but men were not allowed to spend the night in the women's apartments.

### 3 PRISON
In 1974, the American State of Ohio made cheating at golf a punishable offence, with second offenders liable to a prison sentence of up to five years.

### 4 MIRTHLESSNESS
The American College Football coach Woody Hayes never allowed his teams to watch funny films. He said that he had 'never seen a man tackle with a laugh on his face'.

### 5 THE FIRING SQUAD
On 9 November 1980, the Liberian Football XI played a goal-less draw against Gambia. Throughout the game, they had played under the threat of execution if they failed to apply themselves hard enough. But a goal-less draw was considered sufficient, and they lived to play again another day.

**6 A LONGER TRACK**
After the four runners in the men's 200 metres race in the 1904 Olympics had all made three false starts, the judge penalized them by extending the track another metre.

## *Mary Peters'* 5 *Tips to Young Athletes*

1 Train hard and enjoy your sport

2 Don't specialize too soon. Try several events – even the heptathlon or decathlon – before you decide which event is most suitable for you.

3 Join a club with coaches available to help and encourage you.

4 Believe in your ability to succeed. Never say 'I can't'.

5 Be a good loser. Then you can be an even better winner.

## *The Physical Pecularities of 9 Sportsmen*

**1 STEVE DAVIS'S THUMB**
Steve Davis has a double-jointed thumb which curls back to give him one of the firmest bridge hands in snooker.

**2 BILL BEAUMONT'S BOTTOM**
'The biggest bottom in the business? That's right,' says Bill Beaumont, 'the lads say my bum's equivalent to one Erica.'

**3 DUNCAN GOODHEW'S SCALP**
Duncan Goodhew lost his hair when he fell from a tree at his family home in Yapton, Sussex, aged ten.

**4 MARGARET COURT'S ARMS**
Margaret Court's arms are three inches longer than the average woman's.

## 5 DEREK RANDALL'S BODY

'All bones and no meat' is the way Derek Randall describes his own body. 'Bill Taylor, one of the Notts lads, reckons that when they finished putting everybody else together they used all the spare parts to make me. He could be right.'

## 6 BJORN BORG'S PULSE

Bjorn Borg has a pulse rate of 35. The normal pulse rate is between 60 and 80.

## 7 WILLIE SHOEMAKER'S HEIGHT

Willie Shoemaker is only 4ft 11ins. He weighs less than 100lbs, though this is a major increase on the weight at which he was born – $2\frac{1}{2}$lbs.

## 8 GIANT HAYSTACKS' WEIGHT

Giant Haystacks weighs 38 stone. His wife weighs $7\frac{1}{2}$ stone.

## 9 MARVIN HAGLER'S SCALP

Marvin Hagler once explained why he shaved his scalp. 'With four sisters running about the house I could never get my hands on a comb,' he said.

# *Lester Piggott's* 9 *Derby Winners and his Comments on Each of Them*

## 1 NEVER SAY DIE, 1954
'Quite a good horse.'

## 2 CREPELLO, 1957
'One of the great horses I've ridden.'

## 3 ST PADDY, 1960
'A very free horse, always doing everything himself.'

## 4 SIR IVOR, 1968
'My favourite.'

## 5 NIJINSKY, 1970
'That summer he was as good a horse as there's been around since the war. But when he came back in the autumn he wasn't the same.'

6 ROBERTO, 1972
'Put up a very brave performance.'

7 ENPERY, 1976
'Gave me a good ride.'

8 THE MINSTREL, 1977
'The gamest horse of the lot. He really tried right to the end and got there on guts.'

9 TEENOSO, 1983
'He's a very good horse, but it wasn't one of the great Derbys.'

## 7 Members of **Lester Piggott's** Family who have been Involved in Racing

1 **Father-in-law:** The trainer Fred Armstrong.

2 **Father:** Keith Piggott, jockey, and trainer of a Grand National winner.

3 **Mother:** Iris Rickaby, twice winner of the Newmarket Town Plate.

4 **Uncle:** Fred Rickaby, rider of three Classic winners.

5 **Grandfather:** Ernest Piggott, winner of three Grand Nationals.

6 **Great-grandfather:** Tom Cannon, winner of the Derby.

7 **Great-great-grandfather:** John Barham Day, rider of sixteen Classic winners and trainer of seven.

## 8 **Peculiar Places** where Sportsmen met their **Sweethearts**

1 A SOHO RESTAURANT
Henry Cooper met his Italian wife Albina when she was a waitress in a Soho restaurant he frequented.

## 2 IN 'PIRATES OF PENZANCE'

Tom Watson met his wife Linda when they were both in a local production of Gilbert and Sullivan's *Pirates of Penzance* when Watson was thirteen.

## 3 BY THE TABLE FOOTBALL

British Pool Champion Joe Barbara met his wife Hilda when she was playing table football in a Manchester café.

## 4 ON A REVOLVING MACHINE

Kevin Keegan met his wife Jean on a revolving machine known as 'The Waltzer' at a fairground in Doncaster.

## 5 ON TELEVISION

Nancy Lopez married a television sportscaster from WHP-TV, Tim Melton. They first met when he interviewed her on television.

## 6 ON THE DOORSTEP

Jocky Wilson met his wife Malvina when he delivered coal to her door, covered in coal dust from head to toe. At the time, he was on leave from the army and was making extra money as a coalman.

## 7 ON THE TELEPHONE

Barry Sheene met his girlfriend Stephanie Maclean, a former *Playboy* cover girl, after she had seen him on a television documentary she was watching with her husband in 1975. She rang Sheene to borrow his racing leathers for a modelling shot.

## 8 OUTSIDE THE INTERVIEW ROOM

Vijay Amritraj, the Indian tennis star whose name had previously been linked with Farrah Fawcett and Cheryl Ladd, announced his marriage to Shyamala Wenceslaus in January 1983. Shyamala had been selected from one hundred and fifty other prospective brides after interviews with Amritraj's parents. 'We both could have got out of the marriage if we wanted to,' said Shyamala, 'but it didn't take us very long to decide we were right for each other.'

## 5 *Poems* by Sportsmen

### 1 TONY JACKLIN

I'm never happy when I'm not with you
When I'm away I'm always blue
Words can't say how much I care
It's everything when I know you're there
Stay by me all of my life
My friend, my lover, my woman, my wife.

with love Tony

(*To his wife, Vivien*)

### 2 JOHN SNOW

'Anne'

Tomorrow is already here
In the evening of today
For though the path is not lit ·
I'm moving on my way.

The presence which is now
Cannot, unlike the mind,
Be carried to tomorrow's
Richer fields you'll find.

So the kiss is left
The touch withheld undone
For the tears you cry will dry
In tomorrow's warmer sun.

### 3 DEREK DOUGAN

If you think you are beaten you are
If you think you dare not, you won't
If you like to win, but you think you can't
It's almost certain you won't.

If you think you'll lose, you're lost
For out of this world we find
Success begins with a fellow's will
It's all in the state of mind.

## 4  JOE BUGNER

Ali has goofed before and he'll goof again
This is the year of the younger men
The time is now and truth must be told
Muhammad Ali is too bloody old!

(*February 1973*)

## 5  GEORGE BEST

If my desperation leaves us
room for hope
My hope is that our love will
see me through
For through that love my
mind will clear
To reveal our children free
of that desperation
I love you.'

(*To his wife Angie, after she had left him for the fourth time, August 1979*)

## 3 Sportsmen who Used to be **Policemen**

1  Ray Reardon

2  Geoff Capes

3  Chris Dean

## 11 Sporting **Predictions** which Proved Wrong

1  **'I've got no chance.'**
Lester Piggott, aged eighteen, to his father before setting off to win the
1954 Derby on Never Say Die.

2 **'I had dinner with Mark on Saturday night and he told me my job was safe.'**

Manager Ken Craggs, twenty-four hours before being sacked by Charlton Athletic chairman Mark Hulyer in 1982.

3 **'Billie Jean King left Wimbledon yesterday for the last time.'**

Ann Jones, writing in the *Daily Mail* in July 1973. Billie Jean King has appeared at every Wimbledon since, winning the Ladies' Singles in 1975.

4 **'I make bold to say that I don't believe that in the future history of the world any such feat will be performed by anybody else.'**

The Mayor of Dover to Matthew Webb after the first crossing of the English Channel in 1875. An average of fifteen people now swim the channel on every day of August.

5 **'Jeff Thomson looks like a flash in the pan.'**

Keith Miller writing in 1974. Up to the end of the 1981 season, Thomson had taken 166 wickets in 39 Test matches.

6 **'I doubt if I will ever marry. I think I'm too selfish. I've been wrapped up in myself for too long to get involved with anybody else.'**

Steve Ovett, September 1978. He married.

7 **'I have decided to quit as a full-time Soccer manager four years from now. That statement is not meant to shock people, to stir them up or to frighten them. It is a fact.'**

Brian Clough, 5 November 1978.

8 **'Cousins is a great skater but he's chicken. I don't think he'll win the Olympics because of it.'**

Carlo Fasbi, Robin Cousins' American coach, 1980. Cousins won the Gold Medal.

9 **'After ten minutes of talking to Brian Clough, I knew this was the right move. I'm sure we will get on well.'**

Stan Bowles, on moving from Queen's Park Rangers to Nottingham Forest in December 1979. On leaving in May 1980, he said, 'Clough is a dictator ... He says he's socialist but he's one of the biggest Tories I've known.'

10 **'Goodbye my friend.'**
A priest to Niki Lauda in hospital after his major crash in 1976. 'I nearly had a heart attack,' said Lauda later, 'I wanted someone to help me to live in this world and not to pass into the next.'

11 **'We believe the world will end in 1975. If you study the Bible it will tell you. I have saved enough money till then.'**
Ex-Wolves footballer Peter Knowles, after becoming a Jehovah's Witness in 1969.

## 9 Sportsmen who *Prefer Another Sport*

### 1 REX WILLIAMS
Rex Williams, the World Billiards Champion, prefers snooker. He only plays billiards when a championship is imminent.

### 2 DUNCAN GOODHEW
Duncan Goodhew has said that he prefers bobsleighing to swimming. 'It's the ultimate Big Dipper ride,' he says. 'Swimming would have to go a long way to match it.'

### 3 TOM WEISKOPF
In 1977, Tom Weiskopf chose not to play in the USA Ryder Cup team, because he had been balloted a chance to shoot Rocky Mountain big horn sheep in Canada.

### 4 GARETH EDWARDS
Gareth Edwards prefers fishing to rugger. In August 1976, he admitted his obsession. 'I now know precisely what it must feel like to get hooked on heroin or become a compulsive gambler,' he said. 'I know exactly what it means to be pulled against your will to do something.'

### 5 SAM SNEAD
The American golfer Sam Snead said in 1961 that the only reason he played golf in the first place was so that he could afford to fish and hunt.

## 6 TONY WARD

When Irish Rugby Union International Tony Ward toured London in 1978, he was invited to watch a match that London Irish Rugby Club were playing. He refused, saying, 'How could you possibly go and watch London Irish play on the same day Manchester United were playing Arsenal at Highbury?'

## 7 LEE TREVINO

Boxing is Lee Trevino's first love. 'If I'd been born within walking distance of a gym, I wouldn't mind betting I'd be Welterweight Champion of the World today,' he once said.

## 8 DAVID HODGSON

In 1982, footballer David Hodgson acknowledged that he was more successful with his pigeons than with his football. 'I've got a shelf full of trophies, but most of them are for pigeon racing. It's about time I won a few for football,' he said.

## 9 JONAH BARRINGTON

Jonah Barrington has admitted that he thinks that football is 'the greatest game of the lot'.

# 6 *Presents* Given by Sportsmen

## 1 A DIAMOND RING

In 1977, Muhammad Ali gave Julie Collins, a thirteen-year-old Yorkshire girl who was suffering from Spina Bifida, a diamond ring. 'She's a greater champ than I am,' he said.

## 2 CHAMPAGNE

In October 1978, Peter Shilton admitted that he paid his hairdresser with champagne for all the perms he got from him, because he wouldn't accept money from him.

## 3 A REUNION

In 1968, English bullfighter Henry Higgins arranged for a Spanish mother to fly to London for a reunion with her son, whom she had lost after a five-year court battle. He had read of her case in the newspapers. 'I consider it money well spent,' he commented.

## 4 A DOZEN 42-INCH BRAS

Travelling to Nigeria in 1982 to defend his British and Commonwealth light-middleweight title, 'Bomber' Graham took with him a dozen 42-inch bras. He had been specially asked for this gift by a Nigerian promoter, who wanted them for his wife. In return, he was given a snakeskin handbag.

## 5 A DONATION TO THE WAR EFFORT

In May 1982, Guillermo Vilas donated £7,700 to the Patriotic Fund set up by the Argentine government to aid the Falkland war effort.

## 6 OLYMPIC MEDALS

Steve Ovett lent his Olympic medals to a small boy facing an operation. Unlike most sportsmen, Ovett does not have a trophy cabinet. He donates his trophies to youngsters to compete for at a club level.

## 8 Cases of Sporting *Pride Coming before a Fall*

1 **'I am not convinced Steve is as far out on his own as a lot of people believe, and I aim to prove my point in our semi-final showdown.'**
*Jimmy White on 2 December 1981. The next day he was beaten 9–0 by Steve Davis in the Coral UK Championship semi-final.*

2 **'I really think we will go there and win it.'**
*Kevin Keegan on the World Cup, 17 June 1982.*

3 **'Frazier's got two chances: slim and none.'**
*Muhammad Ali in January 1974. Frazier beat him.*

4 **'This Time (We'll get It Right).'**
*Title of a song recorded by the England World Cup Squad in 1982.*

5 **'Our aim is to win the series 6–0.'**
*Graham Yallop, before the first Test against England, 1978–79. England won the series 5–1.*

6 'I like Arsenal. They've had a great season. And it's very sad for them that they are not going to win the FA Cup.'
*John Toshack, 2 May 1971. Arsenal beat Liverpool 2–1 in the final.*

7 'The difference between me and other athletes who go to the Olympics is that I go to win and they go to compete.'
*David Bedford, 1972. He came sixth in the 10,000 metres.*

8 'We will make them grovel.'
*Tony Greig, before the five-Test series against the West Indies, 1976. The West Indies won 3–0.*

## 13 Extraordinary **Prizes** Awarded to Sportsmen

1 A MAMMOTH PUMPKIN
At the close of the Europa Cup contest in Moscow in August 1975, the Russians named David Wilkie 'Man of the Match' and presented him with a huge pumpkin, almost too large for one man to carry.

2 £6,000, A HOUSE AND A CAR
All the footballers in the Kuwait side were presented with £6,000, a house and a car when they qualified for the 1982 World Cup Finals.

3 A GOVERNMENT POST
The Emperor Caligula (AD 12–41) made his champion racehorse Incitatus first a citizen of Rome and then a senator.

4 £3 A YEAR
If you win the Lonsdale Belt three times you qualify for a pension of £3 a year from the British Boxing Board of Control.

5 £2,500 AND A HORSE RIDE
On winning the £2,500 White Horse Golf Personality of the Year award in February 1983, Sandy Lyle was obliged to ride a white horse through Piccadilly. 'I thought motorbikes were dangerous enough,' he said, 'but this thing really scared me.' He had been insured for £250,000 against falling off and hurting himself.

## 6 £1,000
In 1964, Godfrey Evans won £1,000 on the ITV quiz game, *Double Your Money*, answering questions on his special subject, 'Jewellery'. He gave half his prize money to Rev. David Sheppard's Islington Boys' Club and kept the other half himself.

## 7 A BULL'S EAR
If a matador has exceeded himself in a bullfight, the crowd will wave handkerchiefs at the president, who will signal that a tip of the bull's ear should be presented to him. An outstanding performance merits two bull's ears. Between 1962 and 1964, El Cordobes took home 167 bull's ears.

## 8 £6.10s
For winning the 1927 World Professional Snooker Championship, Joe Davis received the sum of £6.10s.

## 9 FREEDOM
In 1777, Bill Richmond, a black slave in Britain, was awarded his freedom in recognition of his sporting achievements.

## 10 £41,231
In March 1961, a syndicate of twenty-two sportsmen and showbusiness personalities, including Freddie Trueman, Jim Laker, Jimmy Hill, Shirley Bassey, Hughie Green, Donald Campbell, Alma Cogan and Jack Brabham, won £41,231 on the pools.

## 11 A HORSE AND CART
When Spyridon Louis won the Marathon at the 1896 Olympics, King George I of Greece asked him what he would like as a prize. He asked for a horse and cart for the people of his village.

## 12 A FREE PERFORMANCE
It was rumoured that the entire 1927 University of California 'Thundering Herd' Football team had slept with the film actress Clara Bow.

## 13 FREEDOM TO PADDLE, WALK OR TROT
In 1978, Red Rum was granted Official Freedom to Paddle, Walk or Trot on the beach of his home town of Southport, Merseyside.

## *Unexpected **Professions** of 5 Former Sportsmen*

1 **Mark Spitz:** a dentist in Southern California.

2 **Peter Bonnetti:** runs a hotel on the Isle of Mull and is also the island's postman.

3 **Raymond Oppenheimer,** British Walker Cup captain 1951: the world's largest breeder of bull terriers.

4 **Francis Lee:** manufactures toilet rolls and other tissue products, employing seventy people.

5 **Ray Wilson:** an undertaker in Huddersfield.

## *6 **Prudish** Sportsmen*

### 1 JOHNNY MILLER
Johnny Miller once said, 'I keep a good clean body – free of alcohol and the like. I don't want to be cast as a sort of prophet or something. I just want to be a good churchman and to have the chance to lead a good life.'

### 2/3 JAMES HUNT AND KEVIN KEEGAN
In 1981, both James Hunt and Kevin Keegan refused up to £100,000 to pose naked in the American *Playgirl* magazine.

### 4 MUHAMMAD ALI
In 1966, Ali was granted a divorce from his wife Sonji. He said he objected to her tight dresses and short skirts, both of which contravened the rules of his Black Muslim sect.

### 5 IVAN LENDL
Ivan Lendl doesn't approve of on-court smiling. 'If I smile I have to think about smiling and that would break my concentration,' he says.

### 6 SUE BARKER
'I've only been drunk once in my life. Never again. It was awful,' says Sue Barker.

# R

## 8 *Refusals* to Sportsmen

### 1 AMERICAN TELEVISION REFUSE ERIC BRISTOW
In 1980, American cinemas and television refused to take a film about Eric Bristow, called *Arrows*, saying they couldn't understand his cockney accent.

### 2 AN ENGLISH COUPLE REFUSE DAVID SHEPPARD
During the 1962 MCC tour of Australia, the wife of an English couple who lived in Australia suggested to her husband that The Rev. David Sheppard should christen their baby. 'Not likely,' replied her husband. 'In his present form he'd be bound to drop it.'

### 3 GILLETTE REFUSE TO SPONSOR CRICKET
In 1980, Gillette backed out of cricket sponsorship. They said that the public had begun associating them more with cricket than with razors.

### 4 THE GLC REFUSE WOMEN WRESTLERS
For thirty-nine years, the Greater London Council has refused to licence women's wrestling.

### 5 ENGELBERT HUMPERDINK REFUSES LEICESTER CITY
In December 1982, singer Engelbert Humperdink refused an offer to join the board of his home club Leicester City, saying that he was too busy with his singing to devote enough time to the club.

### 6 THE FOOTBALL LEAGUE REFUSE BRIAN CLOUGH
In 1978, Brian Clough asked the Football League if his assistant Peter Taylor could walk alongside him in the Cup Final parade. His request was refused.

### 7 VIC EDWARDS REFUSES EVONNE GOOLAGONG
Evonne Goolagong's manager Vic Edwards refused to go to her wedding in 1975. 'She can either give herself to love or tennis,' he said.

## 8  A caddy refuses Craig Stadler

During the British Amateur Championship at Hoylake in June 1975, Liverpool caddy Jimmy Robertson refused to work any more for Craig Stadler. 'I have had enough,' he said, 'I refuse to be treated like an animal. He asked for it. He's been chucking clubs around all week.'

## 18  Things *Refused* by Sportsmen

### 1  The Chair of Poetry at Oxford University

Following his defeat at the hands of Ken Norton, Muhammad Ali was surrounded by speculation that he would retire from boxing. Around this time, he received an offer from Oxford University to stand for election to their Chair of Poetry. He refused in verse:

> Pay heed, my children, and you will see
> Why this is not the time for university.
> It's not the pay, although that's small
> But I have to show the world I can still walk tall.

### 2  A traditional bat

During the Perth test in 1979, Dennis Lillee came on to the pitch brandishing an aluminium cricket bat. When Mike Brearley objected, the umpire asked Lillee to change bats. He refused and walked off. A few minutes later he reappeared, still holding the aluminium cricket bat. At this point Greg Chappell intervened, and persuaded Lillee to go back to a traditional wooden bat.

### 3  An autograph

When the Yugoslav tennis player Zeljko Franulovic was asked by a young American fan if he would autograph her jeans, he replied, 'I'm sorry but we're not allowed to endorse clothing.'

### 4  Twenty scholarships

Daley Thompson has turned down twenty offers of scholarships from American universities. He dislikes the hypocrisy of pretending to be a student while really being a full-time athlete.

## 5 'CELEBRITY SQUARES'
Barry Sheene once refused an offer to appear on *Celebrity Squares*, the television panel game, saying that he considered it banal.

## 6 ALCOHOL
Muhammad Ali did not allow alcohol at the Los Angeles reception in June 1977 to celebrate his marriage to his third wife.

## 7 ABSENCE
In November 1982, Justin Fashanu refused to obey an order from Brian Clough that he should not appear for work for two weeks. Only after the police had been contacted did he agree to leave the football ground.

## 8 MAGIC POTIONS
In 1970, when the England football squad were about to embark on the World Cup, Sir Alf Ramsey received this letter: 'I, Shariff Abu-baker Omar, am the leading Witch Doctor in East Africa with international repute in football and other matters. I have helped Kenya and Uganda National teams to win Trophies in the past and now offer to extend my help to your English National team.' Sir Alf refused, politely.

## 9 TRAINING ON MONDAYS
When they were both playing for Chelsea, Peter Osgood and Alan Hudson formed a 'Monday Club', refusing to train on Mondays. 'The only thing we exercised,' says Osgood, an enthusiastic drinker, 'was our elbows down the King's Road.'

## 10 A RECORD
In 1966, Nobby Stiles issued a writ seeking an injunction to ban a record called 'We Love You, Nobby Stiles' by Bill Oddie. 'It upset my wife and family,' explained Stiles.

## 11 'SUPERSTARS'
In 1978, Steve Ovett refused to appear on the *Superstars* television programme. 'That Superstars programme!' he complained, 'talented sportsmen being asked to jump through hoops when somebody blows a whistle. I think that cheapens sport. People say it makes sportsmen look human. I think it makes them look fools.'

### 12 A SHAVE
Before they met in the ring, Alan Minter demanded that Marvin Hagler shaved his chin. Hagler refused. 'Only if he shaves his head,' he said.

### 13 A LAS VEGAS BOOKING
In March 1977, Joe Bugner refused to fight Ron Lyle in Las Vegas if a woman's boxing match on the same bill was not cancelled. 'To me it's Women's Lib gone mad,' he said. 'I'm all in favour of a woman being boss in her own home, but they need protecting from this.'

### 14 ALLAN WELLS' 'THIS IS YOUR LIFE'
Frank Dick refused to appear on Olympic Gold Medallist Allan Wells' *This Is Your Life*. Dick, the British National Athletics Coach, said, 'There would have been hypocrisy if I had appeared on the programme.'

### 15 ARTIFICIALITY
Jocky Wilson has always refused to put on a special act for television. 'If my nose needs picking, I'll pick it,' he says.

### 16 THE DRAFT
Muhammad Ali refused to fight in Vietnam. 'I don't have no quarrel with them Vietcongs. The Vietcongs don't call me nigger,' he said.

### 17 CONDOLENCES
During the 1932 Bodyline tour of Australia, after Bill Woodfull had been hit over the heart by a ball from Larwood, the English manager, Pelham Warner, walked up to Woodfull to offer his sympathy, but Woodfull refused it, saying, 'I don't want to see you, Mr Warner. There are two teams out there. One is trying to play cricket and the other is not.'

### 18 A HOMOSEXUAL LIAISON
In his autobiography, *To Hell With Hockey*, Aslam Sher Khan wrote that one coach had asked to sleep with him. 'If not, he made it clear, I would not be selected. I was not.'

## 7 *Religious Leaders* who were Keen Sportsmen

### 1 POPE JOHN PAUL II
Pope John Paul II was once goalkeeper with the Polish amateur team Wostyla.

### 2 ROBERT E. RICHARDS
An American preacher, Robert E. Richards, won the Gold Medal for the Pole Vault in the 1952 and 1956 Olympics. He was known as the Vaulting Vicar.

### 3 PLACIDUS A. SPESCHA
Placidus A. Spescha (1752–1833) was an eccentric Benedictine who spent all his time, when not praying, going mountaineering. Half his fellow monks thought he was mad and the other half thought he was a French spy.

### 4 SAINT CUTHBERT
According to the Venerable Bede, St Cuthbert excelled at jumping, running and wrestling.

### 5 THE FIRST OXFORD BOAT CREW
All the members of the first Oxford boat crew took holy orders; one of them, Charles Wordsworth, became a Bishop.

### 6 THE RIGHT REVEREND DAVID SHEPPARD
The Right Reverend David Sheppard, Bishop of Liverpool, used to play cricket for Sussex and for England. His last game for England was in 1963.

### 7 THE REVEREND LORD FREDERICK BEAUCLERK
In the eighteenth century, the Reverend Lord Frederick Beauclerk admitted making £600 a year from cricket. It was widely rumoured that he earned this amount from backing his opponents.

*. . . and one Religious Leader who wasn't*

Sir Osbert Sitwell once complained of Jesus Christ that 'He was never, well, what I call a sportsman. For forty days he went out in the desert and never shot anything.'

## 9 Sportsmen with **Religious Leanings**

### 1 HENRY COOPER
Henry Cooper became a Roman Catholic before marrying his wife Albina. 'I don't mind telling you, there's one part of being a Catholic that comes hard even to this day,' he says, 'and that's the confessing bit.'

### 2 PETER KNOWLES
In January 1969, Peter Knowles and his wife Jean became Jehovah's Witnesses. 'My problem is going to the ground at 10.30 a.m. and 3.00 p.m. each day for training,' he said. 'This leaves me with insufficient time for bible study.'

### 3/4 JOHNNY MILLER AND BILLY CASPER
Both Johnny Miller and Billy Casper are practising Mormons; they both give ten per cent of their earnings to their church.

### 5 OLLIE CAMPBELL
The Irish Rugby Union fly-half Ollie Campbell never goes into an International without consulting Father Jimmy Moran, his old coach at Belvedere College in Dublin. 'I feel better for talking to him. He is a good friend and I find it helps to keep in touch,' he says.

### 6 LAWRIE MCMENEMY
Lawrie McMenemy is a Roman Catholic. On 11 March 1980 he preached from the pulpit of St John's Church, Alresford, Hampshire. 'I don't think I'll be doing it again,' he said afterwards. 'I was terrified.'

### 7 RODNEY MARSH
In 1967, Rodney Marsh said, 'If I hadn't been a footballer, I'd have been something else. For example, a priest. I mean, something different, something nobody else does.'

### 8 MUHAMMAD ALI
Ali is a member of the Black Muslim sect. Once when Floyd Patterson criticized his beliefs, Ali replied, 'I'll fight Patterson in a winner-take-all bout. I would give my purse to the Black Muslims, and Patterson could give his to the Catholic Church if he is the victor. I'll

play with him for ten rounds. I will pow him. Then after I beat him, I'll convert him.'

## 9 GLENN HODDLE

'As I go down the tunnel, no matter where I am, I make the sign of the cross,' says Glenn Hoddle. 'I do it again as the ref blows his whistle. I'm a Catholic and I remember, in my youth, football always came before church. Now I remind myself what really comes first.'

Hoddle also makes regular visits to a spiritualist called Eileen Drewery, the landlady of The Shark public house in Harlow, Essex. 'I have treated him for about eight different injuries,' says Mrs Drewery. 'I know I'm only an instrument. I've no special gifts. I'm only being used. I've had an affinity for him. I feel he's like my child. I felt that from the word go.'

## 5 *Notable* **Riots** *at Sports Grounds*

## 1 THE NATIONAL STADIUM, LIMA, 1964

With Peru trailing Argentine 1-0 with only two minutes to go, the referee, Eduardo Angel Pazos, disallowed a goal by Peru. This resulted in a mass riot in which 350 people were killed, 1,200 injured and every window in the stadium broken. Before leaving hastily for Montevideo after the match, Mr Pazos said, 'Maybe it was a goal. Anyone can make a mistake.'

## 2 THE THIRD TEST AT KINGSTON, JAMAICA, 1968

With the West Indies 29 runs behind and with 5 wickets still standing, Butcher was caught by Parks. The crowd started throwing bottles on to the field, and carried on despite pleas from Colin Cowdrey and Gary Sobers. Eventually, the police came in with tear gas, but the wind was blowing in the wrong direction and the tear gas went straight for the pavilion and the press box.

## 3 SYDNEY, 1879

In a match between New South Wales and the Lord Harris XI, the Australian crowd started shouting 'Not Out, Go Back' after an umpire had ruled against an Australian batsman. One of the Lord Harris XI riposted by shouting, 'You're nothing but the sons of convicts', whereupon 2,000 spectators stormed the pitch. Lord Harris himself remained steadfastly on the pitch, believing that, according to the rules, if he left the pitch he could have to concede the game. He received a number of kicks but no serious injury. After an hour and a half of this rioting, the game was abandoned.

### 4 THE BLAYDON RACES, 1916
When Anxious Moments, the winner of the Blaydon Races, was found to be carrying a stone less than the specified weight and disqualified, furious backers set fire to the weighing room and the stewards' room, wrecked the bookies' stands, and threw several jockeys into the River Tyne. Following this riot, the Blaydon Racetrack was closed down forever.

### 5 THE FIRST TEST AT PERTH, 1982
When the English team reached a score of 400, twenty people rushed the pitch. Terry Alderman pushed one of them out of his way and was in return struck on the head. He gave chase and rugger-tackled the youth, an unemployed machinist. Lillee and Border helped him pin him down until the police arrived. Other fans began jumping back over the fence. The police charged into them, arresting twenty-five, most of them the sons of English immigrants. During the affray, Alderman dislocated his right elbow. After this riot, the Australian Cricket Board issued a ruling that players should not 'have a go' at spectators invading the cricket pitch. Previously, the code of conduct had stated, 'Players must not assault or attempt to assault an umpire, another player, or a spectator. This code does not apply to any player's conduct towards any spectator trespassing on the ground.'

## 5 Sportsmen who have made *Rude Gestures*

### 1 ALEX HIGGINS
During the 1973 Snooker World Championships, Alex Higgins turned up late for an association inquiry into why he had turned up late for the championship and why he had worn a green evening suit instead of a black one. On leaving the meeting with a fine of £100, he gave the officials a V-sign.

## 2 RUTH CARRIER

After Jimmy Connors had disputed a number of line calls while playing Peter McNamara in Toronto in February 1982, he asked for the lineswoman, 51-year-old Ruth Carrier, to be removed. 'I was ready to walk off, then I thought, "Damn it, you brat", and I gave him a one-fingered salute,' said Miss Carrier later.

## 3 DEREK RANDALL

After fielding at Headingley in 1977, Derek Randall was officially admonished by the chairman of the selectors, Alex Bedser, for scratching the word 'TITS' on the turf with his spikes when a well-endowed young woman had passed along the boundary edge.

## 4 IAN CHAPPELL

During the World Series Cricket Supertest in 1979, the Sydney crowd booed when Ian Chappell dropped two catches. On catching a third successfully, Chappell gave the crowd a double V-sign.

## 5 HARVEY SMITH

Having ridden Mattie Brown to victory at Hickstead in 1971, Harvey Smith made a V-sign towards the Devil's Dyke balcony, from which had erupted a cheer when his horse had knocked a pole down. The directors, who had been situated in the Devil's Dyke balcony, were not amused, and disqualified Smith later that day. Two days later they relented, though they did not seem to be impressed by Smith's excuse that it was merely a V for Victory.

## *10 People who have Managed to Change the **Rules** of Sports*

## 1 PRESIDENT THEODORE ROOSEVELT CHANGES THE RULES OF AMERICAN FOOTBALL

In 1905, there were no fewer than eighteen deaths and 159 serious injuries in American College Football. When President Roosevelt saw a particularly nasty photograph of one such injury in a newspaper, he demanded that the rules of the game be changed, which they were, allowing the ball to be passed forward.

## 2  DENNIS LILLEE CHANGES THE RULES OF CRICKET

In February 1980, after Dennis Lillee and a backer had spent £400,000 on developing an aluminium cricket bat, Lords revised Law 6 to stipulate that 'the blade of the bat shall be made of wood'.

## 3  GEORGE LAMBTON CHANGES THE RULES OF RACING

In 1903, George Lambton, Lord Derby's trainer, who was acknowledged as one of the most honest men in racing, doped his horses in order to prove to the Jockey Club that rules should be introduced to prevent it. In the same year, doping was forbidden.

## 4-7  THE BRASENOSE FOUR CHANGE THE RULES OF ROWING

At the 1868 Stewards Cup at Henley, the Captain of the Brasenose Four ordered the cox to jump out of the boat at the beginning of the race. The Brasenose crew won but was immediately disqualified. However, the next year there was a race for coxless fours, and after 1873 all fours were coxless.

## 8  BILL VEECK CHANGES THE RULES OF BASEBALL

In a characteristically bizarre attempt to raise his team's score, Bill Veeck, the owner of the St Louis Browns baseball team, introduced to his ground an adjustable-height fence. He raised it when his opponents went in to bat and lowered it for his own team. A rule banning such devices was swiftly added to the books.

## 9  GEORGE EASTMAN CHANGES THE RULES OF FOOTBALL TRANSFERS

In 1963, George Eastham of Newcastle United challenged his club's right not to allow him a transfer. Up until then, all rights in a transfer belonged to a club, but the High Court abolished this system.

## 10  BELINDA PETTY CHANGES THE RULES OF JUDO REFEREEING

In August 1980, Judo referee Mrs Belinda Petty complained to an industrial tribunal of sex discrimination after the British Judo Association had placed a ban on women refereeing all-male events at a national level. During the tribunal, the British Judo Association staged a fight refereed by a woman, to demonstrate the trouble involved. Another woman referee, Mrs Elisabeth Viney, backed their ban, saying, 'It is rather like appointing a female lavatory attendant to a male toilet.' Nevertheless, Mrs Petty was given the unanimous verdict.

# S

## 4 Sportsmen who have **Saved** a Stranger's Life

### 1 BRIAN CLOUGH
In 1980, Brian Clough talked a Nottingham woman, Mrs Barbara Terry, out of a hunger strike at the Nottingham Hospice for Incurables. Clough left a players' meeting and spoke with her on the phone for half an hour. 'He has given me a reason for living. I have never felt such tenderness. Mr Clough is a truly wonderful man,' said Mrs Terry.

### 2 PETER ALLISS
Peter Alliss's recorded voice roused Simon Deakin, of Widnes in Cheshire, from a coma in 1981.

### 3 MUHAMMAD ALI
In January 1981, Muhammad Ali talked a 21-year-old man from jumping out of a ninth floor Los Angeles office window. He then drove him to a police station in his Rolls-Royce. 'I'm going to put him in college and find him a job,' said Ali, 'I promised to help him with his life if he didn't jump.'

### 4 STEVE DAVIS
After two weeks in a coma, Phyllis Mould from Eccles regained consciousness when Steve Davis entered her hospital room in January 1983. He had agreed to visit her after hearing that she idolized him. 'Steve's been a real tonic,' said one of the nurses.

## 6 Sportsmen's Views on **Sex** before Sports

### 1 ILIE NASTASE
'You know what they say about it being bad for your game. Well, I can tell you it's rubbish. Sex before tennis brings me luck.'

2  MUHAMMAD ALI
Ali wouldn't make love to his wife for six weeks before a major fight.

3  JIMMY CONNORS
Jimmy Connors sees both sides of the question. 'As far as Jimmy and I go, it depends on the tournament,' says his wife Patti. 'Tennis is a mental game and you need all your concentration. If you think that little bit is going to give the extra edge, then abstain.'

4  JOHNNY FAMECHON
Australian sportsman Johnny Famechon used to tie a piece of string around the end of his penis, believing that an involuntary nocturnal emission would weaken his sporting performance the next day.

5  GUILLERMO VILAS
At one point in his tennis career, Vilas gave up sex for a year in order to improve his game.

6  TOMMY DOCHERTY
When he was manager of Rotherham United, Docherty banned his players from sex between Wednesday and Saturday before a big match.

## 8 Products Endorsed by **Barry Sheene**

1  Brut Aftershave

2  Marlboro Cigarettes

3  Daf Trucks

4  Mazda Cars

5  Travel Cruiser Mobile Homes

6  Shell Oil

7  Yamaha Motorcycles

8  AKAI Hi-Fi

## 7 *Remarkable* **Shots** *in Sports*

### 1 THE FACTORY WINDOW SMASH HIT
In 1902, Australian batsman Victor Trumper broke a window in a shoe factory 150 yards away. The owners of the factory kept the window in its broken state as a memorial.

### 2 THE REBOUNDING GOLF SHOT
In the St Andrew's Amateur Golf Championships in 1930, a ball hit by Bobby Jones was heading for the rough, but instead hit a spectator's ankle and rebounded on to the green. Jones was the eventual winner of the Championship.

### 3 THE HOLE IN ONE FOOTBALL SHOT
In the Charity Shield game of 1967, Tottenham Hotspur's goalkeeper Pat Jennings's clearance went first bounce over the head of Manchester United goalkeeper Alex Stepney and into the back of the net.

### 4 THE 2,640-YARD GOLF SHOT
In 1962, an Australian meteorologist, Nils Lied, drove a golf ball 2,640 yards. He was aided by his surroundings – he drove it across the ice in Antarctica.

### 5 THE 37-MILE CRICKET SLAM
At a match in Hull in July 1876, W.G. Grace hit a ball by mistake into a travelling railway truck. It was eventually picked up thirty-seven miles away in Leeds.

### 6 THE GULL-BATTERING SHOT
In the Sixth Test between England and Australia at Adelaide in 1971, a shot by Keith Stackpole hit a seagull, thus slowing the ball down and losing him two runs. The gull was treated for a broken leg.

### 7 THE GOB-STOPPING GOLF SHOT
In June 1971, Robert Wilson drove a ball from the tenth tee of the Quinidi Golf course. It struck a tree, passed through the windshield of a moped and lodged in the driver's mouth.

## 12 Sportsmen who **Smoke**

Lester Piggott (Havana cigars)

Barry Sheene (Gauloises)

Bob Taylor (a pipe)

Rosie Casals (cigars)

Geoff Capes (snuff)

Ian Botham (cigarettes)

David Bryant (a pipe)

John Francome (cigars)

Chris Brasher (30 cigarettes a day)

Joe Brown (cigars)

Ossy Ardiles (cigarettes)

Shirley Strong (cigarettes)

*. . . and one Horse*

Loh (marijuana)
(Following a very poor run by his three-year-old colt Loh in the 1976 2,000 Guineas, Reg Akehurst claimed that the horse had been doped with marijuana.)

## 9 **Songs** to Learn if You Want to be a Football Supporter

1 'When the Saints Go Marching In' (*Southampton*)

2 'The Blaydon Races' (*Newcastle United*)

3 'The Pompey Chimes' (*Portsmouth*)

4 'I'm Forever Blowing Bubbles' (*West Ham United*)

5 'You'll Never Walk Alone' (*Liverpool*)

6 'John Brown's Body' (*Tottenham Hotspur*)

7 'Abide With Me' (*Wembley anthem*)

8 'Follow, Follow, We Will Follow Rangers' (*Rangers*)

9 'Sure It's A Grand Old Team To Play For, It's A Grand Old Team To Know' (*Celtic*)

*5 Sportsmen who Felt **Sorry** for Themselves*

1 **'I trained for four years just for this two-minute trip and I only got a few seconds.'**
*Konrad Bartelski in February 1976, having fallen near the top of the slope in the Men's Downhill Championship.*

2 **'I was sent to Crewe and Carlisle by managers, and to Coventry by my wife.'**
*Stan Bowles, in June 1976.*

3 **'If a fox is completely brilliant he finds himself a hole and hides. If his position is discovered, he is dug up and thrown to the hounds. But a football manager hasn't even got a hole to hide in.'**
*Brian Clough.*

4 **'John Bond has blackened my name with his insinuations about the private lives of all football managers. Both my wives are upset.'**
*Malcolm Allison.*

5 **'Every day I feel like quitting. Every time in fact that somebody hits me. But every time I hit it is a thousand dollars.'**
*Sugar Ray Leonard, in March 1980.*

## *11 Top Sporting* **Speeds**

1 **A sprinter:** 27 mph over 100 yards

2 **Henry Cooper's left hook:** six inches in 48 thousandths of a second, or 30 mph

3 **A racehorse:** 60 mph over a 5-furlong race

4 **A racing pigeon:** 90 mph

5 **A cricket ball:** 100 mph

6 **A table-tennis ball:** 120 mph

7 **A skier:** 124 mph

8 **A water skier:** 128 mph

9 **A tennis ball:** 140 mph

10 **A golf ball:** 250 mph

11 **A racing car:** 257 mph (*Porsche 917/30*)

## *6 Sportsmen who are Not the* **Sporting Type**

1 PETER SHILTON
In 1978, Peter Shilton admitted that he drove sixty miles to have his hair permed. He added that he gave his hair a herbal shampoo twice a week.

2 SUGAR RAY LEONARD
Sugar Ray Leonard has admitted that, 'The first thing I do when a fight is over is to run to the mirror to see what damage has been done.'

3 MUHAMMAD ALI
Muhammad Ali dyes his hair black.

4 MICHAEL PARKINSON
Michael Parkinson has admitted that he was disqualified from a boxing bout at school on the grounds of cowardice.

5 ZAMORA

The Spanish International goalkeeper Zamora hated dirt and mud. Occasionally he would bring a broom on to the field and, when it was safe, he would tidy up the goalmouth.

6 JOE BUGNER

Late in 1982, Joe Bugner's mother, Margrit, telephoned her son and told him that he looked 'like a big poofter' on television.

*. . . and all Baseball Players*

By 1907, American baseball players had become so exasperated by visiting Britons saying that in fact baseball was an English girls' game called Rounders, that a special seven-man committee including two senators was set up to investigate the matter. They eventually issued a report stating categorically that baseball had been invented in 1839 on a field in Cooperstown. But the credibility of the committee, and the manliness of baseball, were both overthrown when a diligent librarian, Robert Henderson, came across the following sentence in Jane Austen's *Northanger Abbey*, published in 1798:

'. . . and it was not very wonderful that Catherine, who had by nature nothing heroic about her, should prefer cricket, baseball, riding on horseback and running about the country at the age of fourteen, to books . . .'

Henderson also discovered that The Rules of Rounders, published in *The Boy's Own Book* in 1829, corresponded exactly with The Rules of Baseball, published in the *American Book of Sports* in 1834.

Despite all this evidence, a National Museum of Baseball was established on the Cooperstown field in 1939 as part of the Centenary celebrations.

*The 3* **Stallions** *from which All Thoroughbreds are Descended*

1 **The Byerley Turk** (*captured at Buda in 1688*)

2 **The Darley Arabian** (*bought in Aleppa in 1704*)

3 **The Godolphin Arabian** (*foaled in the Yemen in 1724*)

(*There are now roughly three-quarters of a million thoroughbreds in the world*)

## 5 Memorable Sporting **Streaks**

### 1 THE HELMETED STREAKER OF TWICKENHAM
On 23 April 1974, Michael O'Brien, an Australian, streaked across the Twickenham ground during the half-time interval of the England v. France Rugby international. A policeman escorted him from the pitch, having first placed his helmet over Mr O'Brien's offending parts.

### 2 THE ZIG-ZAGGING STREAKER OF MONTREAL
During the closing ceremony of the 1976 Montreal Olympics, a man ran to and fro between the colourful dancing gymnasts.

### 3 THE SORE STREAKER OF LORD'S
On 4 August 1975, a man streaked across Lord's cricket ground and hurdled over both sets of stumps. Greg Chappell brandished his cricket bat and gave him a whack on the bottom as he passed.

### 4 THE MUSICAL STREAKER OF WEMBLEY
On 8 May 1976, a man wearing only a pair of pants climbed on to the crossbar at Wembley Stadium before the Rugby League Cup Final and from this vantage point began to conduct the band.

### 5 THE WELL-ENDOWED STREAKER OF TWICKENHAM
On 2 January 1982, Miss Erica Roe streaked topless across the pitch at Twickenham during a Rugby International between England and Australia. Bill Beaumont, turning round to see what was diverting the attention of his players from his half-time tactical talk, was heard to exclaim, 'God, they're big, aren't they?' The following Monday, Miss Roe returned to her job in a Petersfield bookshop.

## 8 Sportsmen's **Superstitions**

### 1 MARTINA NAVRATILOVA
Martina Navratilova knocks on her racket before she plays. 'Borg is something like that,' she says. 'He doesn't shave at Wimbledon. I have decided not to shave either. Perhaps I will grow a beard too.'

## 2 ALAN KNOTT
Alan Knott likes to touch the tops of the stumps in between balls.

## 3 JOHN·MCENROE
John McEnroe hates playing tennis on any Thursday 12th. As a boy, he ran his bicycle into a tree on a Thursday 12th.

## 4 THE PRINCE DE CONDE
In the eighteenth century, The Prince de Conde built the luxurious Grands Ecuries at Chantilly for his racehorses to live in. He made it so comfortable because he believed in reincarnation and was sure that he would return to earth as a thoroughbred.

## 5 BETTY STOVE
Betty Stove never steps on the alley lines when she changes ends.

## 6 BILLIE JEAN KING
Billie Jean King always takes her baths in the same bathtub whenever she is at Wimbledon.

## 7 ANN JONES
Ann Jones always considered it lucky if the umpire was wearing yellow socks. In 1969, she persuaded umpire Laurie McCallum to wear them, and went on to become only the second Briton to win the Ladies Singles title at Wimbledon since the war.

## 8 SANDY LYLE
Golfer Sandy Lyle usually wears blue in important championships. 'I like blue,' he says, 'I usually seem to be in blue when I win.'

## 5 Extraordinary Racing *Swindles*

### 1 THE NON-EXISTENT MEETING AT TRODMORE
In 1880, at Easter, a particularly busy time for racing, the editor of *Bell's Life* (which has since amalgamated with *Sporting Life*) received a letter from the Secretary of the Trodmore Hunt giving details of runners and riders at the Trodmore Race Meeting on Easter Monday. The Secretary of the Hunt offered to telegram the results for Tuesday's

newspaper. The overworked editor accepted the invitation with thanks, and Tuesday's *Bell's Life* carried the results. Only when another newspaper, copying the results from *Bell's Life*, printed a price as 7-2 rather than 5-2, and bookmakers attempted to contact the Trodmore Secretary to verify the price, did they discover that there was no such person, no such hunt and no such meeting. By this time they had already paid out a large amount of money, and the culprit was never discovered.

### 2 THE SEVERED LINES AT BATH
At Bath in 1953, over £50,000 was bet on the winning horse Francasal at 10-1. After the race, bookmakers were furious because they had been unable to transfer bets via the blower to the racecourse, so that they couldn't shorten the odds. Police later arrested two men who had been acting suspiciously with a ladder, and from them discovered that the horse had in fact been the champion Santa Amaro and that telephones lines to Bath had been specially cut. The Welsh gang was sent to prison and when its head, Gomer Charles, was released, he was murdered by robbers who had heard that he had large sums of money in his house.

### 3 THE BOGUS COMMENTARY AT MELBOURNE
At Melbourne in 1939, a gang cut all the radio cables before the last race, except for one, on which they broadcast a bogus commentary a few minutes after the race had been run. In those few minutes, the name of the winning horse had been phoned through to accomplices, who then backed it. Many bookies lost thousands of pounds.

### 4 THE SWITCHED HORSES AT EPSOM
In the 1844 Derby, the winner Running Rein was in fact a much better horse called 'Maccabeus'. Mr Goodman Levy, who owned both, had switched them and had then backed the winner to gain him £50,000. As a precaution, he had given the horse to a friend, Alexander Wood, before the race. His plot came unstuck when the bookmakers became suspicious and refused to pay out, and the prize money was also withheld. When the innocent Wood didn't get his prize money, he went to court. When the defence gave evidence that dye had been sold to Goodman Levy, the judge summoned him. But by this time both Levy and his horse had disappeared.

## 5   THE DOPED HORSE AT EPSOM

In the very same 1844 Derby, William Crockford, the owner of the co-favourite, Ratan, discovered that his trainer's son had backed a horse called 'Ugly Buck'. Crockford became certain that 'Ratan' had been doped, but he died only three days later and was thus unable to check up on his suspicions.

# T

*12 Bizarre **Tactics** Employed by Sportsmen*

1 BITING
A boxing match held at the Miami Beach Convention Centre in 1973 had to be stopped when both contenders began biting each other. One of them was later rushed to hospital to be given a tetanus injection.

2 SPEAKING WELSH
To keep their plans private, and perhaps also to inject fear into the opposing team, Gareth Edwards and Barry John used to speak in Welsh on the pitch.

3 POINTING UPWARDS
W.G. Grace used chattily to point out something in the sky to his opponents, thus blinding them with the sun.

4 HUMILIATING YOUR CLUB
American golfer Fuzzy Zoeller has admitted that sometimes he switches putters, 'just to let the other one know I can get along without him.'

5 REJECTING SHOES
The winner of the Marathon at the Rome Olympics, Abebe Bikala, ran barefoot the whole way. A member of the Imperial Guard of Emperor Haile Selassie, it was only his third ever Marathon.

6 CHALKING YOUR HANDS
Eric Bristow puts chalk on his hands to stop himself sweating.

7 BARGING THE GOALIE
In the 1958 Cup Final, the Bolton Wanderers centre-forward scored a goal by charging the Manchester United goalkeeper between the posts while he was holding the ball.

## 8 STOPPING FOR NOTHING

In the Paris–Brest–Paris cycling marathon of 1928, Australian Hubert Opperman pioneered a method of relieving himself without stopping his bike. On coming to a downhill stretch, he would freewheel and urinate at the same time. For this he was voted 'Sportsman of the Year' by readers of the French *Auto* magazine, beating all French contenders.

## 9 FIBBING

Bill Shankly once revealed that to bolster his team's confidence before a big match he would go into the dressing-room and say, 'Christ, I've seen the other team coming in, boys. They've been out on the tiles all night. They're frightened to death.'

## 10 EMPLOYING A MIDGET

Bill Veeck, the notorious owner of the ailing baseball team The St Louis Browns, once fielded a midget called Eddie Gaedel, who was only 3 ft 7 ins tall. This made a mockery of one of the rules of baseball that requires the ball to be pitched between the batter's knees and his armpits. Depending on the batter's stance, this usually allows a space of about thirty inches, but in Eddie Gaedel's case the space was only one and a half inches. After four misplaced pitches, the batter is allowed to go straight to first base. Following four misplaced pitches, Gaedel went to first base and was immediately replaced by a substitute. The next day Bill Veeck was banned permanently from having anything to do with baseball. 'Discrimination against little people,' he complained.

## 11 BAITING

After the 1978 tour of Australia, Botham explained that he used to enjoy trying to anger Australian fast bowler Rodney Hogg. 'I used to get Hoggy going when, at the end of that stooping, knees-bend run-up of his, I would shout down the wicket, "I know I'm good, sport, but there's no need to get down on your knees and pray".'

## 12 SNITCHING A WHIP

On 12 March 1964, when Terry Biddlecombe was riding The Pouncer in the Juliet Hurdle at Stratford, he accidentally dropped his whip. As he turned into the straight, he offered a fellow jockey £10 to borrow his whip. When the jockey refused, Biddlecombe snatched it, going on to win the race by a head.

## 7  *Historic Sporting* **Telegrams**

### 1 'That's the only way to show the bastards best wishes Brian Barbara and the kids'

Sent by Brian Clough to his friend Geoff Boycott after Boycott had scored a century on the first day of a County Championship season.

### 2 'We can help you'

Sent by 'Conservation of Manpower', an alcoholics group, to George Best after they had read of his drinking bouts in the Press. He accepted their offer.

### 3 'Because of your disgusting gesture the directors and I have disqualified you'

Sent by Douglas Bunn to Harvey Smith in 1971, after the notorious V-sign episode. Two days later, Bunn changed his mind and reinstated Smith.

### 4 'Before leaving a bunker a player should carefully fill up all holes made by him therein'

Sent by The Royal and Ancient Golf Club to Captain Alan Shepard in 1971. The commander of Apollo 14, Shepard had hit two golf balls with an ironheaded club when he was on the moon.

### 5 'Chiron is at the crossing'

Sent by American footballer Frank Augustus from his deathbed to his former team-mate George Adee, December 1925.

### 6 'You have done for Australian cricket what the Boston Strangler did for door-to-door salesmen'

Sent by Jack Birney, Australian MP, to Geoff Boycott during the Second Test match in Perth, 1978. Boycott had spent an especially long time scoring half a century.

### 7 'Keep corpse on ice till innings declared'

Sent by Dr E.M. Grace, coroner brother of W.G. Grace, to his office in Bristol. They had sent him a telegram at the Oval, demanding his prompt return to Bristol to preside over an inquest.

***Mark Thatcher's*** *5 Favourite Racing Cars in the World*

1 Ferrari 512M

2 Porsche 917K

3 Williams FW07C

4 Osella PA8

5 Chevron B16

***Daley Thompson's*** *Desert Island Discs*

1 'Abraham, Martin and John', by Marvin Gaye

2 'You've Got a Friend', by James Taylor

3 'Sho'nuff Must Be Love', by Heatwave

4 'Together', by O.C. Smith

5 'For The Good Times', by Al Green

6 'The Best Days of My Life', by Rod Stewart

7 'Unchained Melody', by George Benson

8 'Three Times a Lady', by The Commodores

*Luxury:* A guitar

*Book: The Collected John Wyndham*

*9 Violent* ***Threats*** *by Sportsmen*

1 **'One day I'll smash him for that. I'll tear his legs off.'**
Adrian Street talking about Bill Ross after Ross had ripped off Street's gold lamé trousers in front of television cameras.

2 **'Le quiero arrancar la cabeza.' ('I want to tear off his head.')**
Roberto Duran before fighting Sugar Ray Leonard at Wembley in
November 1980. His wish was denied him: he lost.

3 **'Do that again and I'll break your jaw.'**
Alan Evans to Jocky Wilson at the Embassy World Darts Championship in January 1982. He accused Wilson of clicking his darts together
as an irritant. 'The trouble with Alan Evans is that he just can't take
a beating,' retorted Wilson.

4 **'You bloody cannibal, I'll get you for that.'**
English hooker Alvin Ackerley to Australian Ian Walsh, who had
bitten his hand so hard in a scrum that it was bleeding. The next year
they met again, and Ackerley showed Walsh the scar he still had. 'We
had a good laugh over it,' commented Walsh.

5 **'I'll tell you what I'd like to do to Davis. I'd like to stick his
cue ...'**
Alex Higgins on Steve Davis in an interview in the *Daily Mirror*, 14
December 1981.

6 **'I'll give him talking lessons and boxing lessons. What he
needs most is falling down lessons. That big black bear ain't
gonna beat me, 'cos I'm gonna float like a butterfly, sting like
a bee.'**
Muhammad Ali in February 1964, on Sonny Liston.

7 **'If I don't win this tournament I'm going to nail him to the
wall.'**
Lee Trevino on his caddie, Willie Aitchison, in 1972. He had earlier
said, 'Willie here doesn't even know how to spell golf, and he's trying
to tell me what club to use.'

8 **'I want to hit you, Bailey. I want to hit you over the heart.'**
Peter Heine to Trevor Bailey in 1956.

9 **'I'll chase that son of a bitch Borg to the ends of the earth.
I'll be waiting for him. I'll dog him everywhere. Every time he
looks round he'll see my shadow.'**
Jimmy Connors, 1978.

## 8 Unexpected *Titles* Awarded to Sportsmen

1 BRITISH CHILDREN'S MOST POPULAR PERSONALITY
Awarded to Big Daddy, after a 1980 publishing poll had discovered that British children preferred him to his closest competition, who included Snoopy, Kevin Keegan, Debbie Harry, J.R. and Lassie.

2 MALE HEAD OF THE YEAR
Awarded in 1978 to Peter Shilton by the National Hairdressers Federation.

3 PC 184
Ray Reardon's title when he was a policeman in Stoke-on-Trent.

4 FILM CENSOR
An appointment given to Ron Clarke, the Australian athlete, in 1970 by the Liberal Government. Mr Chipp, the minister responsible for appointing him, said that Clarke represented the man in the street. 'I know nothing about films,' said Ron Clarke.

5 PAPAL KNIGHT
Awarded to Henry Cooper by the Vatican in appreciation of his charity work.

6 SEXIEST LEGS IN FOOTBALL
Awarded to Glenn Hoddle's legs after a vote by thousands of women in a 1982 newspaper poll.

7 A BARD IN THE GORSEDD OF BARDS
Awarded to Gareth Edwards in 1976. Introducing him in a ceremony to the Inner Circle of the Royal National Eisteddfod, the Druid of Wales, the Reverend Bryn Williams, described Edwards, somewhat inaccurately, as 'the Wizard of the Round Ball'.

8 LOUDEST GRUNTER
Awarded to Jimmy Connors, after a sound meter at Wimbledon in 1981 had recorded his pre-serve grunt at 69 decibels in the second set of his match with Tony Giammalva. McEnroe reached 53 decibels, and Fritz Buehning 56.

## 6 Comments by **Torvill and Dean** on Each Other

1 'It's rare for us to quarrel off the ice, sometimes only because I am a very tolerant person. Few people, for instance, would stand for Chris's back-seat driving.'
*Torvill on Dean.*

2 'She is the Chancellor of the Exchequer, and when we are abroad I rarely have a pfennig or a franc in my pocket. Does that sound ominously like a hen-pecked husband?'
*Dean on Torvill.*

3 'I sometimes think it is like a marriage, really, apart from the fact that we spend the nights separately.'
*Torvill on Dean.*

4 'I think we fell in love and out again, but it is difficult to be sure because we were so young at the time.'
*Dean on Torvill.*

5 'I cannot imagine getting married to Chris at the moment. Don't bet against it, though.'
*Torvill on Dean.*

6 'It is a strange relationship we have, a mystery to most people, including ourselves.'
*Dean on Torvill.*

## 5 Superstitions of **Torvill and Dean**

1 Both of them tie their left boot first.

2 Chris Dean always steps on to the ice with his left foot first.

3 Chris Dean always carries a pair of gloves in his bag. So far, he has never been known to use them.

4 Jayne Torvill takes three little Paddington Bears with her to all competitions.

5 Chris Dean wears the same pair of St Michael's pants in Cambridge Blue whenever he competes.

## 11 Curious **Training** Methods

### 1 LIVING IN A DEEP FREEZE
David Hempleman-Adams prepared for his solo trip to the North Pole in Spring 1983 by pitching a tent in a commercial deep freeze in the Bejam Freezer Centre in Farnborough, where temperatures reached minus 40c.

### 2 MAKING IT EASY
Ray Reardon trained himself by playing with marbles rather than billiard balls on a billiard table. 'Of course, then the pockets were far too big, and the marbles would fly in from anywhere,' he says. 'But that's the way to learn to play something. Make it easy for yourself.'

### 3 PRACTISING IN THE DARK
Tennis player Jeff Boroviak practises his service in the dark, believing it is a major factor in improving his play.

### 4 JOINING THE MILK FLOAT
Former British gymnast Suzanne Dando used to train by joining her milkman boyfriend Paul Baker on his rounds, leaping on and off the float to deliver the milk.

### 5 BEING STRANGLED
At the age of fifteen, British Judo Champion Brian Jacks was trained by being strangled by Japanese trainer Kisaburo Seki to the point of unconsciousness and then, on coming round, being strangled again. 'After a while I was able to count the number of times,' he says. 'Once it happened eleven times in a row.'

### 6 SKIING ON A GOLF COURSE
Canadian swimmer Steve Podborski learnt to ski on a golf course in Toronto.

### 7 Taking it out on the family
Big Daddy has said, 'I'll wrestle with anyone – even my wife and daughter if I can talk them into it.'

### 8 Chopping trees
Muhammad Ali trained for his fight with Ken Norton in 1973 by cutting down trees. 'Every time I chop down a tree, I yell "Ken Norton!"' he said.

### 9 Training during sleep
In Summer 1978, cricketer Derek Randall announced that he planned to sleep in a crash helmet for a fortnight to get used to wearing one.

### 10 Mind over matter
When Malcolm Allison was manager of Manchester City he photo-copied the message, 'Every day in every way I am getting better and better, physically and mentally.' He gave a copy to each player, telling them to repeat it to themselves twenty times in the morning and twenty times at night.

### 11 Motorway skiing
In July 1975, police stopped François Demarquette as he was being towed along the hard shoulder of the M4 on a pair of skis by a car driven by his wife. The skis had been fitted with wheels. The couple said in a letter to the court that the skis had been designed to simulate travelling by snow. They were fined £25 each and had their driving licences endorsed.

## 10 Sportsmen who have been **Turned Down**

### 1 Andy Gray
Brian Clough and Peter Taylor considered signing Andy Gray from Aston Villa in 1977. A major factor in their decision against him was that they didn't approve of him being a part-owner of a nightclub.

### 2 Daley Thompson
As a teenager, Daley Thompson went for a trial at Fulham Football Club, but was turned down.

### 3  TONY GREIG
Tony Greig was turned down for National Service in South Africa because of his epilepsy.

### 4  FRANK BRUNO
Heavyweight boxer Frank Bruno was originally turned down by the British Boxing Board when he wanted to go professional, because he failed their eyesight test.

### 5  SIR ROGER BANNISTER
Sir Roger Bannister's first ambition was to row for Oxford in the Boat Race. But when he applied to join the team he was laughed at for being too thin. Instead, he took up athletics and went on to become the first man to break the four-minute mile.

### 6  ALAN BALL
As a teenager, Alan Ball was turned down by Bolton Wanderers. He went on to become a member of England's World Cup winning team in 1966.

### 7  LORD HESKETH
A month before his company brought out a £4,495 motorbike, Lord Hesketh failed his motorcycle riding test in Northampton on a 250cc Suzuki. He was failed for poor gear changes and driving too slowly.

### 8  BARRY JOHN
Just four years before making his debut in the Welsh National Rugby team, Barry John was turned down for the Welsh Schools side.

### 9  BILLY WRIGHT
The Manager of Wolves, Major Buckley, told Billy Wright that he was too small to be a professional footballer. Wright went on to win 105 caps for England, 90 of them as captain.

### 10  KEVIN KEEGAN
In August 1969, Brian Clough and Peter Taylor travelled to Southend to watch Kevin Keegan play for Scunthorpe. They had been considering signing him, but they eventually decided that he was too small and hadn't the right experience. Two years later, Liverpool signed him for £30,000.

*The 7 Sports Stars who have Lasted less than Four Years in **Madame Tussaud's** before being Melted Down*

1 Bobby Moore      1971–1974

2 Colin Cowdrey    1968–1971

3 Virginia Wade     1978–1979

4 Jim Clark         1965–1967

5 David Hemery     1968–1971

6 Don Revie        1976–1977

7 Roger Bannister   1955–1958

# U

## 6 Sporting **Understatements**

1 **'You give a little, you take a little.'**
*Graham Price, Welsh prop forward, on his return from Australia, having had his jaw broken by a punch from Steve Finnane.*

2 **'We had some misfortune here and a lot of bad luck.'**
*John Tipper, manager of the British Speed Skating Team, on his return from the Winter Olympics in 1980. In nine races, the six British contestants had only beaten two Chinese, a Mongolian and an Italian.*

3 **'It's a marvellous thing to play for England. You get a few quid, it's nice for the family, and you wear three lions on your chest.'**
*Derek Randall.*

4 **'I was lucky to have the right horse on the right day.'**
*Bob Champion, after winning the Grand National on Aldaniti.*

5 **'It was all a bit of high spirits.'**
*John Conteh, having ripped wall lights from their sockets, destroyed a number of plants and shattered three chairs while staying free at an hotel in Newcastle-under-Lyme during a charity walk in December 1980.*

6 **'I meant to make him a jockey and it came off. It doesn't often, but it certainly came off with him.'**
*Keith Piggott on his son Lester.*


## 11 **Unsophisticated** Sportsmen

1 FRED TRUEMAN
Dining at the University Arms in Cambridge, Fred Trueman spent a

long time studying the French menu. Eventually, he pointed to the bottom of the menu and said to the waiter, 'Aye, and ah'll have that for sweet.' He had chosen Jeudi le Douzième Mai.

## 2 BABE RUTH
After Babe Ruth, the legendary baseball star, had been rehearsed for a radio broadcast to say, 'The Duke of Wellington's historic remark that the Battle of Waterloo was won on the playing fields of Eton ...', he in fact said on air, 'As Duke Ellington once said, the Battle of Waterloo was won on the playing fields of Elkton.'

## 3 IAN BOTHAM
As journalist Dudley Doust was travelling in Ian Botham's car through Somerset, he turned the radio to Radio 3. 'None of that Radio 3 stuff,' said Botham, 'I'm Ian Botham, not Mike Brearley.'

## 4 A COUNTERFEIT STUDENT
Scared that they would lose an inter-varsity match against Trinity College, Dublin, Cambridge fielded a professional rugger player. Everything went well until the formal dinner afterwards. The professional who was by no means an academic, was following instructions and simply saying, 'yes' or 'no' to every question his neighbour asked him. But then his neighbour asked him what he studied at Cambridge. 'Sums', he replied.

## 5 TOM WEISKOPF
During the Muirfield British Open in 1972, Tom Weiskopf was relaxing watching television after completing his first round when a woman about forty years old entered the lounge of his hotel. Without looking up from the television, Weiskopf asked her if she played golf. She said that she had played a few rounds, and that her father had been very keen on it before his death.

'What did your father do?' asked Weiskopf.

'He was King of England,' replied Princess Margaret.

## 6 MUHAMMAD ALI
'Gee, that's a mighty swell pad,' said Ali, on first seeing Buckingham Palace.

## 7 ALBERT GRIFFITHS
The Australian boxer Albert Griffiths was unable to read or write, but

would nevertheless pretend to read newspapers and telegrams, frequently holding them upside down.

## 8 DIZZY DEAN
Dizzy Dean, an ex-baseball player who then became a sportscaster in St Louis, so mangled the English language that the Missouri Teachers' Association asked for him to be fired. They particularly objected to his using 'slud' as the past tense of 'slide'. 'Well, what do they expect me to say? Slidded?' asked Dean.

## 9 GENE TUNNEY
In April 1928, the go-ahead Professor Phelps of Yale University asked Gene Tunney, the professional boxer, to address his literature class. Tunney began by telling the class that 'Shakespeare was a sport', followed this by admitting that he had read *A Winter's Tale* ten times before he could understand it, and concluded by talking about combat in *Troilus and Cressida*. Newspaper columnist Heywood Brown commented, 'Harvard, I trust, will counter by asking Babe Ruth to tell the boys at Cambridge just what Milton has meant to him.'

## 10 DEREK RANDALL
Derek Randall is the first and only person to have asked for 'The Sun Has Got His Hat On' when he was a guest on *Desert Island Discs*.

At a house party during the MCC tour of India in 1976–77, Randall was handed caviar. 'The blackcurrant jam tastes of fish to me,' he commented.

## 11 JAMES THORPE
In the 1912 Stockholm Olympics, James Thorpe, a Fox Indian, won the Decathlon and the Pentathlon and was seventh in the Individual Long Jump. After his victories, he was presented to the King of Sweden, who told him that he was the greatest athlete in the world.

'Thanks, King,' replied Thorpe.

# V

## The 4 Most **Atrocious Verses** from Songs Recorded by Sportsmen

1 'One hundred and eighty, one hundred and eighty,
Everyone tries for the maximum score,
Three treble twenty, with three arrows needed,
If you miss the bed, you can try once more.'

*From 'One Hundred and Eighty', sung by Bobby George and Jocky Wilson, 1981*

2 'When we arrived people said
The Aussies would leave us for dead
But we knew we would prove them wrong
And that's why we're singing this song
Oh! The feeling is great
For losing is something we hate.'

*From 'The Ashes Song', written by Brian Johnston and sung by the English Cricket team, 1972. Total royalties: £53.86p*

3 'Everyday we're gonna say we love you,
Leeds, Leeds, Leeds,
Everywhere, we're gonna be there,
We love you,
Leeds, Leeds, Leeds.'

*From 'Leeds, Leeds, Leeds,' sung by Leeds United, 1972*

4 'For when he goes in to bat
He knocks every record flat
For there isn't anything he cannot do.
Our Don Bradman, every Aussie dips his lid to you!
Our Don Bradman, now I ask you is he good?
Our Don Bradman as a batsman he is certainly plum pud!'

*From 'Don Bradman – Is he any good?', by Jack O'Hagan, 1930. It sold 40,000 copies in three days in one record shop alone.*

## 8 Acts of **Violence** by Sportsmen

### 1  THE BITE
'If a finger gets in my mouth during a game there's only one reason – the bloke wants to rip my face. The quickest way to stop that is to close your teeth.' This was the method described by Johnny Raper, the captain and coach of the St George Australian Rugby team in 1969.

### 2  THE CIRCULAR LEG
In 1974, Ben Gilbert, the right back for Mawgan United was sued by Perranporth's Ron Grundy for breaking his leg in five places, thus losing Grundy ten months' work as a pump attendant. 'I was going for the ball,' said Gilbert in his defence. But Mr Justice Mars-Jones ordered Gilbert to pay Grundy £4,000 compensation.

### 3  THE KILLING
In 1843, two Frenchmen, Lenfant and Mellant, quarrelled over a game of billiards and drew lots to see who should throw the red ball at the other. Mellant won, hurled the ball at Lenfant's forehead and killed him instantly.

### 4  THE BROKEN RIBS
One passage of Johnny Sample's autobiography, *Confessions of a Dirty Ballplayer*, reads: 'I came into him, elbows and knees flying. Now I could have jumped over him touching him just enough to down the ball. But I didn't. And the result was that I broke three of his ribs.' Sample was a member of the New York Jets American Football team.

### 5  THE MURDER
In 1972, an entire soccer team was arrested and imprisoned after a linesman had been attacked and kicked to death during a game in Cordoba, Argentina.

### 6  THE AMATEUR BOUT
Five days before their official fight in January 1974, Joe Frazier and Muhammad Ali wrestled on the floor of a television studio following an argument. It took a dozen men to pull them apart. For their behaviour they were later fined £2,000 by the New York State Athletic Commission.

## 7 THE FAMILY MUGGING

In September 1982, referee Brian Harper was attacked by five members of the Compton family as he blew the final whistle on a village football match in which Great Somerford had lost 6-1. Great Somerford had recently received an award for fair play. Later in court, Peter, Michael, Kenneth, Hugh and Kevin Compton all admitted conduct likely to cause a breach of the peace. They were all fined, and Peter and Michael were banned for seven years from playing football by the Wiltshire FA.

## 8 THE MASS VIOLENCE

Within six minutes of the opening of the second half of the England-Australia Rugby League match in Sydney in 1954, the Australian half-back, Keith Holman, had been knocked unconscious and Ray Price had been sent off. The Australian captain then started fighting an English player. Another Australian joined in, and soon almost every player was punching another player. The referee, Aub Oxford, abandoned the game, saying, 'If this is Rugby League, I'm finished with it', and never refereed a match again.

## *Vital Statistics* of Big Daddy

*Weight:* 25 stone

*Age:* 50

*Chest:* 62 inches

*Shoes*: Size $13\frac{1}{2}$

*Wife's Comment:* 'He doesn't fit into the bath. We hose him down in the garden.'

# W

## 5 Reasons for Sportsmen **Walking Off**

### 1 AN IMPERTINENT SPECTATOR

After Cliff Thorburn had lost 5-0 to Graham Miles in the third round of the 1981 Jameson Whisky International Open Snooker Championship, the two of them played an exhibition match. Straightway, Thorburn potted a red. This prompted a spectator to shout, 'Why didn't you pot like that in the match?' – whereupon Thorburn walked out of the auditorium.

### 2 AN IMPERTINENT INTERVIEWER

In May 1963, in the run-up to his fight with Henry Cooper, Muhammad Ali walked out of a television interview with David Coleman when Coleman said, 'I must admit, I'm a Cooper fan – and so are most of the British people. And I think you talk too much.' As he left, Ali, said, 'I don't have to be on your programme. You aren't doing me a favour. I should be in bed resting. I'm going.'

### 3 A SICK FRIEND

Tom Weiskopf walked out of the Westchester Classic tournament in 1976 because his playing partner Bert Yancey was having a nervous breakdown. Despite a $3,000 fine, Weiskopf did not reveal his reason for leaving until Yancey had been committed to a mental home. 'I knew he was going to crack up any minute', he said, 'and I could not bear to watch it.'

### 4 THE CALL OF NATURE

At a banquet in Leeds attended by Harold Wilson, Brian Clough who had been called upon to respond to the toast, said, 'I've been sitting here for two and a half hours and before I respond to anyone I'm going to the toilet.' He then left the banquet for eleven minutes. He later commented, 'If in future they want a puppet to get up and say something to please everybody, I suggest they invite Basil Brush.'

5 GRUMPINESS

After he had been defeated by John McEnroe in the 1981 US Open at Flushing Meadow, Bjorn Borg walked off the court without waiting for the presentation.

## The 13 **Weight Categories** for Professional Boxing

| | | | |
|---|---|---|---|
| 1 | Light-Flyweight | up to | 108 pounds |
| 2 | Flyweight | up to | 112 pounds |
| 3 | Bantamweight | up to | 118 pounds |
| 4 | Super-Bantamweight | up to | 121 pounds |
| 5 | Featherweight | up to | 126 pounds |
| 6 | Junior Lightweight | up to | 130 pounds |
| 7 | Lightweight | up to | $134\frac{1}{2}$ pounds |
| 8 | Light-Welterweight | up to | 140 pounds |
| 9 | Welterweight | up to | 147 pounds |
| 10 | Light-Middleweight | up to | 154 pounds |
| 11 | Middleweight | up to | 160 pounds |
| 12 | Light-Heavyweight | up to | 174 pounds |
| 13 | Heavyweight | over | 174 pounds |

## **Jocky Wilson's** 5 Top Darts Players in the World

1 **John Lowe:** 'The most consistent player in the world since 1979.'

2 **Eric Bristow:** 'I have to admit that I've got a soft spot for Eric ... I think we have one thing in common: we are both either brilliant or just below par.'

3 **Jocky Wilson:** 'I have been described as fat, boozy and toothless. That's pretty accurate, I guess.'

4 **Cliff Lazarenko:** 'Nobody puts them in as neatly as 20-stone Cliff.'

5 **Dave Whitcombe:** 'Dave has a casual, relaxed-looking style. He takes no prisoners.'

### *Wimbledon* Men's Singles Champions since 1972

1972: Stan Smith (*beat Ilie Nastase*)

1973: Jan Kodes (*beat Alex Metrevelli*)

1974: Jimmy Connors (*beat Ken Rosewall*)

1975: Arthur Ashe (*beat Jimmy Connors*)

1976: Bjorn Borg (*beat Ilie Nastase*)

1977: Bjorn Borg (*beat Jimmy Connors*)

1978: Bjorn Borg (*beat Jimmy Connors*)

1979: Bjorn Borg (*beat Roscoe Tanner*)

1980: Bjorn Borg (*beat John McEnroe*)

1981: John McEnroe (*beat Bjorn Borg*)

1982: Jimmy Connors (*beat John McEnroe*)

1983: John McEnroe (*beat Chris Lewis*)

### *Wimbledon* Women's Singles Champions since 1972

1972: Billie Jean King (*beat Evonne Goolagong*)

1973: Billie Jean King (*beat Chris Evert*)

1974: Chris Evert (*beat Olga Morozova*)

1975: Billie Jean King (*beat Evonne Cawley*)

1976: Chris Evert (*beat Evonne Cawley*)

1977: Virginia Wade (*beat Betty Stove*)

1978: Martina Navratilova (*beat Chris Evert*)

1979: Martina Navratilova (*beat Chris Evert*)

1980: Evonne Cawley (*beat Chris Evert-Lloyd*)

1981: Chris Evert-Lloyd (*beat Martina Navratilova*)

1982: Martina Navratilova (*beat Chris Evert-Lloyd*)

1983: Martina Navratilova (*beat Andrea Jaeger*)


## *How to **Win** – 12 Sportsmen's Secrets for Success*

### 1 MUHAMMAD ALI ON BOXING

'I'll tell you my secret. It is this. I make any man who comes against me lose his confidence. There he was wingin' away and all the time I was talkin' to him sayin', "Hit harder, George. That was the best you got? They told me you had body punches but that don't hurt even a little bit. Harder sucker, swing harder. You the champion and you gettin' nowhere. Now I'm gonna jab you." Then pop! I'd stick him with a jab ...'

(After his win against George Foreman in 1974)

### 2 JOHNNY MILLER ON GOLF

'You've got to turn yourself into a material as soft as putty, and then just sort of slop the clubhead through. You'll hit much farther and with less effort.'

### 3 BRIAN CLOUGH ON BEING A FOOTBALL MANAGER

'It doesn't matter if the players like you or dislike you. It's when they respect you that they play for you.'

### 4 ROBERT MORLEY ON BETTING

'If in the paddock the owner is surrounded by a herd of young children, don't back his horse. But if the owner is accompanied by a beautiful lady, plunge to the hilt.'

## 5 Chris Lloyd on Tennis
'Desire is the key. I don't feel it consistently, but when I have it I can't be beaten.'

## 6 W. G. Grace on Winning the Toss
'When you win the toss, bat. If you are in doubt, think about it, then bat. If you have very big doubts, consult a colleague, and then bat.'

## 7 Alan Evans on Darts
'I need six or seven pints and half a dozen trips to the gents before I'm ready to play.'

## 8 Tommy Docherty on Football
'If you have the ball you should have ten attackers. Only when the other side has it should you have ten defenders.'

## 9 Rod Laver on Tennis
'Don't compose eulogies to yourself when you get ahead.'

## 10 Bob Willis on Cricket
'I aim at the batsman's chin so that he'll hook up and sky a catch.'
(After breaking Rick McCosker's jaw)

## 11 Babe Saharias on Golf Driving
'I just loosen my girdle and let 'er rip.'

## 12 Lee Trevino on How To Avoid Lightning
'Hold up a one-iron and walk. Even God can't hit a one-iron.'
(Trevino still suffers from backache after being struck by lightning in 1976)

### 6 Good Things to Say upon **Winning**

1 'I'm over the moon!'

2 'Magic!'

3 'I'm chuffed.'

4 'Just amazing. Can't describe it.'

5 'He carried me all the way. I just had to sit on him.'

6 'It's the greatest moment of my life!'

## *13 Sportsmen's Reactions to* **Winning**

### 1 DEIFICATION
When Ali beat Ron Lyle in 1975, he said, 'I must be the greatest. Am I immortal too?'

### 2 AFFECTION
When Steve Ovett won the 800 metres at the 1980 Olympics he spelt out the letters I L Y (I Love you) to the television cameras, and they were seen by his girlfriend Rachel back in Britain. He also likes to wave when he wins. 'I'm called all sorts of names for doing it,' he says, 'but what happens when I don't do the arm-waving? They say I was struggling. So I can't win either way.'

### 3 ELEVATION
When Lee Trevino won the US Open in 1967, he said, 'Yesterday I was a poor Mexican. From now on I'm going to be a rich Spaniard.'

### 4 OVER-EMOTION
When his 25–1 horse Knight of Love won at Cheltenham in 1982, John Manners ducked under the rail and ran towards him, waving his hat in the air and cheering. For this he was fined £50 by the stewards for improper conduct. 'I admit to being emotional and headstrong and don't mind being called Mad Manners, but I am not really Bad Manners,' he commented later.

### 5 EXTRACTION
Jocky Wilson lost his false teeth when he gave a yell to celebrate a victory, and they dropped from his mouth and smashed on the floor.

## 6 CELEBRATION
Vitas Gerulaitis has vowed that if ever he wins Wimbledon he will move his bed into a nightclub and stay there for a week.

## 7 VALEDICTION
'No more chip butties for me,' was John Conteh's comment upon winning the World Light-Heavyweight title in 1974.

## 8 EXHILARATION
On winning the Masters in 1979, Fuzzy Zoeller threw his putter high into the air. 'I threw the putter so high that someone said they saw it going over Denver. I had done something I'd been fantasizing over since I was ten years old.'

## 9 DEDICATION
Having recovered from cancer to win the 1981 Grand National, the first thing Bob Champion said on passing the post, was, 'I rode this one for all the patients still in hospital. And for the people who look after them. My only wish is that my winning shows them there is always hope and that all battles can be won.'

## 10 REHABILITATION
Shortly after having his Gold Medal placed over his head at the 1980 Winter Olympics, Robin Cousins transferred it to the head of his mother Jo.

## 11 FASCINATION
After beating Dino Dennis in the third round at Alexandra Pavilion in February 1983, Joe Bugner said, 'I knew it was over before he hit the floor. His eyes rolled right back and came back down again just like a fruit machine.'

## 12 DISSENSION
After winning five Gold Medals in the 1980 Winter Olympics, Eric Heiden said, 'Five Gold Medals? What can you do with them? Heck, I'd rather have a warm-up suit. At least you could wear that.'

## 13 SUBMERSION
At the 1956 Melbourne Olympics, when Vyacheslav Ivanov, winner of the Single Sculls, was awarded his Gold Medal, he hurled it into the air with such abandon that it landed in Lake Wendouree. Ivanov

dived in after it but couldn't find it. A duplicate was specially minted for him.

## 5 *Comments by Sportsmen on* **Winning**

1 **'Winning isn't everything, it's the *only* thing.'**
*Vince Lombardi, American football coach.*

2 **'I get so desperate to win that I shake.'**
*Eric Bristow.*

3 **'Coaches at College say you have to want to kill your opponent if he makes a shot, instead of saying, "Hey, nice going, fella." You've got to go around thinking that playing golf, and winning, is the biggest thing in the world. Well, it may be one of the nicest things in the world, but it sure ain't the biggest. No way, Baby.'**
*Fuzzy Zoeller.*

4 **'Everyone asks you all the time, "Are you going to win?" Well, how on earth do you know if you're going to win or not?'**
*Lester Piggott.*

5 **'I can't remember anyone ever asking, "Who came second?" can you?'**
*Ray Reardon.*

## **Words of Wisdom** *from 7 Sportsmen*

1 **'I lip-read and I watch people's faces. They're more expressive than horses' faces, but not so reliable.'**
*Lester Piggott.*

2 **'You're not a real manager unless you've been sacked.'**
*Malcolm Allison.*

3 'There are only three things worth doing in life – eating, drinking and making love, and if you speak during any of them you are wasting your time.'
*Yachtsman Uffa Fox, when asked by Brian Johnston how his marriage worked when his French wife could speak no English and he could speak no French.*

4 'I believe that if a man wanted to walk on water, and was prepared to give up everything in life, he could do it. He could walk on water. I am serious. I really, practically, believe that.'
*Stirling Moss.*

5 'I don't like people, you see. In fact I hate them. But kids and animals – I can communicate with them.'
*Adrian Street.*

6 'I'm not just involved in tennis, I'm committed. Do you know the difference between involvement and commitment? Think of ham and eggs. The chicken is involved, the pig committed.'
*Martina Navratilova.*

7 'Never catch a loose horse. You could end up all day holding the f------ thing.'
*Lester Piggott, in conversation with Jeffrey Bernard.*

9 **Wives'** *Comments on their Sporting Husbands*

1 HILARY BEAUMONT ON BILL
'He looks so rough and tough, but he's ever so gentle. He calls me dwarf and picks me up with one hand.'

2 JO CHAMPION ON BOB
'He's just a big softie really.'

3 BARBARA THORBURN ON CLIFF
'I'm so lucky with Cliff. He is wonderful. I trust him completely and he has never given me cause to worry. He lets me read all his fan mail, and when I ask if he has noticed any particularly attractive girl fan he

always says, "Honey, you know I don't look." He makes me feel very
secure.'

### 4  LIZ RANDALL ON DEREK
'When we were first married Derek used to throw tea cups behind his
back and catch them. That's one way he got out of doing the dishes.'

### 5  SUZY SPITZ ON MARK
'I thought he'd probably had so much adulation and was so famous
that he'd be wrapped up in himself. Instead I found a sweet, lovable,
easy-going guy.'

### 6  EUNICE CRABTREE ON HER HUSBAND, BIG DADDY
'I wouldn't want Shirley any other way. He's just my big, cuddly
gentle giant. He wouldn't hurt a fly.'

### 7  MRS BOWLES ON STAN
'My husband never cuddles me like that.' (On seeing a newspaper
photograph of her husband clasping a topless model called Jenny)

### 8  MELODY BUGNER ON JOE
'I don't believe Joe could ever really love a woman. He's too much in
love with himself.'

### 9  MARLENE BUGNER ON JOE
'He's a big, gentle bear of a man.'

## 7 Sportsmen who are Not Mad About **Women**

### 1  RAY REARDON
'If I had to make the choice between staying married and playing
snooker, snooker would win.'

### 2  KEITH DELLER
'The girls are the worst. At one time they would turn up their noses at
me, but now they flock around, putting their arms around me and
kissing me.'

### 3 ERIC BRISTOW
'They tend to get a bit silly. They giggle a lot and tend to get on your nerves.'

### 4 BRIAN CLOUGH
'Footballers' wives should be like small boys – seen and not heard.'

### 5 MUHAMMAD ALI
'My toughest fight was with my first wife, and she won every round.'

### 6 TONY SIBSON
'Women – if anything frightens me, they do.'

### 7 STAN BOWLES
'If I had the choice of a night with Raquel Welch or going to a betting shop, I'd choose the betting shop.'

*. . . and one sportsman who thinks women really do like him*

'They see a powerful, dominant and attractive man who can't be pushed around by anybody . . . everybody that their husbands aren't. But in turn they don't want to make their feelings obvious – so they slag me off and *pretend* they don't like me.' – *Giant Haystacks*

## *Ian Wooldridge's* 9 Greatest Sporting Moments that he has Witnessed

1 Franz Klammer's Olympic Gold Medal in the Downhill, Innsbruck, 1976.

2 James Hunt's World Championship Grand Prix victory, Mount Fuji, Japan, 1976.

3 Mary Peters' Pentathlon Gold Medal, Munich Olympics, 1972.

4 Ken Barrington's 143 for England v. West Indies in Trinidad against the hostile bowling of Charlie Griffith, 1967–68.

5 Muhammad Ali's knock-out of George Foreman, in Zaïre, 30 October 1974.

6 Ted Dexter's innings of 70 v. West Indies at Lord's, 1962.

7 Sebastian Coe's 1,500 Metres win at the Moscow Olympics, 1980.

8 Niki Lauda's third place in the Monza Grand Prix.

9 Filbert Bayi's 1,500 Metres win in the Commonwealth Games, New Zealand, 1974. Both Bayi (Tanzania) and John Walker (New Zealand) broke the existing world record in times of 3:32:16 and 3:32:52 respectively.

## *8 Sportsmen who couldn't Adapt Well to the Big Wide* **World**

### 1 CLIFF JONES
Cliff Jones, former Spurs and Wales footballer, invested all his money in two butcher's shops that went bust.

### 2 JOHN CONTEH
In December 1980, John Conteh opened a restaurant called 'J.C.', built around the theme of his initials. It was decorated with pictures of Julius Caesar, Julie Christie, Jimmy Carter, Jaffa Cakes and many others. In August 1981, it closed down, losing Conteh approximately £100,000.

### 3 PETER STOREY
In 1977, Peter Storey, the former Arsenal and England football star, was fined £65 and told that he had behaved like a little boy after being found guilty of butting a 65-year-old lollipop man on the head. In 1979 he was fined £180 for selling alcohol after hours. Later the same year he was given a suspended jail sentence for running a brothel and living off immoral earnings. He had been running an agency called 'The Calypso Massage Service' in Leytonstone. In 1980 he was found guilty of financing a swindle involving fake gold sovereigns, and soon afterwards of having stolen two cars in 1978. He now says, 'I've made a complete mess of my life, I had the chance to make something good out of it, but I blew it all on birds and booze. But at least I've had a great time doing it.'

## 4 DAVID WEBB

Dave Webb, the former Chelsea footballer, ran into trouble with his business interests and had to close down his hairdressers and his boutique. He also had to scale down his second-hand car business, an action which involved sacking his sister.

## 5 RON YEATS

Ron Yeats, the former Liverpool footballer, lost his life earnings when his petrol tanker business went bankrupt.

## 6 JESSE OWENS

Champion runner Jesse Owens was expelled from the American Athletics Union for refusing to compete in a Swedish tour. This cut him off from his living, and he was eventually reduced to freak show racing, against horses and motorcycles.

## 7 ALBERT GRIFFITHS

After his retirement, the legendary Australian boxer Albert Griffiths, best known as 'Griffo', used to stand on pennies in bars, promising drinks to anyone who could hit him on the jaw. Though he never moved off the penny, he rarely lost. Thus he became an alcoholic. Eventually he died in poverty in New York, begging money on 42nd Street.

## 8 RANDOLPH TURPIN

On 16 May 1966, Randolph Turpin former World Middleweight Champion, committed suicide by shooting himself. He had got into debt and owed the Inland Revenue a considerable amount of money. He left a suicide note to his wife saying, 'I hope you will forgive me for this terrible thing.'

In his funeral address, the Rev. John Hazeldean said, 'At the height of his career, Randolph was surrounded by those who regarded themselves as friends and well-wishers. But he was deserted by as many as he lost his position and money.'

*The Countries which have Knocked England Out of the **World Cup** Finals*

1950  Spain

1954  Uruguay

1958  Russia

1962  Brazil

(*1966 England won*)

1970  West Germany

(*1974  England didn't qualify*)

(*1978  England didn't qualify*)

1982  Spain


*The England **World Cup** Winning Team of 1966*

1  Gordon Banks (*Leicester City*)

2  George Cohen (*Fulham*)

3  Ray Wilson (*Everton*)

4  Nobby Stiles (*Manchester United*)

5  Jack Charlton (*Leeds United*)

6  Bobby Moore (*West Ham United*)

7  Alan Ball (*Blackpool*)

8  Geoff Hurst (*West Ham United*)

9  Bobby Charlton (*Manchester United*)

10  Roger Hunt (*Liverpool*)

11  Martin Peters (*West Ham United*)

WORLD CUP FINAL SCORE: England 4, West Germany 2

## *World Cup Winners* since *1930* (*with host country in brackets*)

1930 Uruguay (*Uruguay*)

1934 Italy (*Italy*)

1938 Brazil (*France*)

1950 Uruguay (*Brazil*)

1954 West Germany (*Switzerland*)

1958 Brazil (*Sweden*)

1962 Brazil (*Chile*)

1966 England (*England*)

1970 Brazil (*Mexico*)

1974 West Germany (*West Germany*)

1978 Argentina (*Argentina*)

1982 Italy (*Spain*)


## *10 Key Words in* **Wrestling** *Slang and their Meanings*

1 **To die:** To appear to be losing, thus arousing the crowds

2 **A crowbar:** A wrestler who grips too tightly

3 **A knock-off man:** A wrestler who is ordered to lose

4 **A blade:** A razor blade used in the ring to draw blood

5 **Thermos:** A mask

6 **The groin:** The ring

7 **Cheap heat:** Getting the crowd worked up by gimmicks

8 **To shoot:** To fight to win

9 **To do your gregory:** To appear to hurt your neck

10 **To do your haystack:** To appear to hurt your back.

# Y

## 7 *Sportsmen who Started **Young***

### 1  JAMES HUNT
James Hunt learnt to drive a tractor at the age of 9.

### 2  GARETH EDWARDS
Gareth Edwards, who captained Wales aged 20, was the youngest International Rugby captain ever.

### 3  LESTER PIGGOTT
Lester Piggott won his first race – a three-furlong gymkhana at Wantage – aged 6. He rode his first professional winner aged 12, and won his first Derby aged 18.

### 4  EAMONN COLLINS
Aged 14, Eamonn Collins became the youngest player ever to appear in a Football League club competition when he appeared as a substitute for Blackpool.

### 5  STEVE CAUTHEN
Steve Cauthen won his first race aged 16, had won 487 races and more than six million dollars by the time he was 17, and won the US Triple Crown aged 18.

### 6  BEVERLEY WILLIAMS
Beverley Williams represented Great Britain at diving aged 10, in 1967. She retired aged 18.

### 7  MARJORIE GESBRING
Aged 13, Marjorie Gesbring won the Gold Medal for Springboard Diving at the Berlin Olympic Games in 1936.

## 8 Sportsmen's Memories of Themselves when they were **Younger**

### 1 GEORGE BEST
'I was very unattractive and I remember the birds teasing me. They used to shout, "Look at that skinny, ugly sod" when I walked past them.'

### 2 GIANT HAYSTACKS
I had a terrible time at school, with other kids ridiculing me. It hurt me deeply. I couldn't match their cruel tongues, so I retaliated in the only way I knew – with my fists. I never lost a fight, but I still couldn't win. I got in trouble for picking on kids smaller than me. But there wasn't anybody even half as big as me.'

### 3 KENNY ROBERTS
'I was always captain of football, baseball, soccer; whatever we did at sports, because I would beat up anyone who disagreed with me.'

### 4 DUNCAN GOODHEW
'Ten is a cruel age to lose your hair, especially when you're at boarding school. There I was, bald and unable to spell. I was just a stupid oddity.'

### 5 JOCKY WILSON
'When I was a wee boy I ate too many sweets and made matters worse by not cleaning my teeth ... I lost my last tooth aged 28.'

### 6 TRACY AUSTIN
'When I was ten all I ever dreamed of was playing at Wimbledon with the greats, and having my ears pierced.'

### 7 JOHNNY MILLER
'If I could putt now like I could when I was twelve, there wouldn't be anything I wouldn't win.'

### 8 BIG DADDY
'As I left the ring they would burn me with cigarettes, kick me, hit me with handbags and umbrellas, and I didn't give a damn. I just felt elated.' (Up until 1976, Big Daddy was the unpopular 'Battling Guardsman.')

# INDEX

# INDEX

# Index

# INDEX

# INDEX

Nicholson, Bill (*football manager*) 28
Nijinsky (*racehorse*) 151
Nicklaus, Jack (*golfer*) 26, 48, 70, 82, 85, 112
Nicklaus, Jack Jr (*son of Jack Sr*) 70
Nixon, President Richard 76
No Bombs (*racehorse*) 58
Northumberland, Duke of (*boxing patron*) 94
Norton, Ken (*boxer*) 24, 164, 192
Nurmi, Paavo (*runner*) 93

O'Brien, Michael (*streaker*) 180
O'Connor, Frank, (*rugger player*) 101
Oddie, Bill (*comedian*) 165
Oerter, Al (*discus thrower*) 100
O'Hagan, Jack (*singer*) 198
Oldfield, W.A. (*cricketer*) 26
Omar, Shariff Abubaker (*witch doctor*) 165
Onishenko, Boris (*pentathlete*) 34
Oppenheimer, Raymond (*golfer*) 162
Opperman, Hubert (*cyclist*) 185
Orwell, George (*writer*) 68
Osgood, Peter (*footballer*) 17, 79, 165
O'Sullevan, Peter (*commentator*) 40
Outlette, Dennis (*boxer*) 98
Ovett, Steve (*athlete*) 19, 59, 70, 85, 98, 103, 105, 147, 156, 159, 165, 206
Owens, Jesse (*athlete*) 89, 92, 213
Oxford, Aub (*rugger referee*) 200
Oyama, Masutatsu (*karate champion*) 139, 140

Packer, Kerry (*cricket entrepreneur*) 76
Paget, Dorothy (*racehorse owner*) 75
Paisley, Bob (*football manager*) 11, 36
Palmer, Arnold (*golfer*) 2
Parkinson, Michael (*chat show host*) 6, 136, 178
Pascoe, Alan (*athlete*) 102
Patterson, Floyd (*boxer*) 45, 168
Patton, General 91
Pazos, Eduardo Angel (*football referee*) 169
Peel, Bobby (*cricketer*) 18
Peters, Jim (*athlete*) 39
Peters, Martin (*footballer*) 214
Peters, Mary (*athlete*) 19, 150, 211
Petronelli, Goody (*manager of M. Hagler*) 93
Petty, Mrs Belinda (*judo referee*) 172
Phelps, John (*rowing umpire*) 137
Phelps, Professor 197
Philippides (*founder of Marathon*) 57
Phillips, Hazel (*tennis player*) 67
Phillips, Mark (*rider*) 44
Pickering, Ron (*commentator*) 24
Pietri, Dorado (*athlete*) 39, 63
Piggott, Ernest (*jockey*) 152
Piggott, Keith (*jockey and trainer*) 152, 195
Piggott, Lester (*jockey*) 43, 105, 121, 132, 136, 151, 152, 155, 176, 195, 208, 209, 216
Pinturischio (*racehorse*) 123
Pirie, Gordon (*athlete*) 19

Player, Gary (*golfer*) 31
Pocock, Nick (*cricketer*) 47
Podborski, Steve (*swimmer*) 191
Price, Graham (*rugger player*) 195
Pringle, Derek (*cricketer*) 44
Pycroft, Rev. James (*cricket historian*) 134

Quadri, Jean-Louis (*footballer*) 66
Quatro, Suzi (*singer*) 45

Radley, Clive (*cricketer*) 72
Rafferty, Max (*state superintendent*) 49
Ramsey, Sir Alf (*football manager*) 106, 165
Rand, Mary (*athlete*) 19
Randall, Derek (*cricketer*) 10, 41, 72, 73, 83, 85, 101, 105, 111, 137, 151, 171, 192, 197, 210
Randall, Liz (*wife of Derek*) 210
Raper, Johnny (*rugger player*) 199
Ratan (*racehorse*) 183
Ratjan, Herman (*athlete*) 36
Rattigan, Sir Terence (*playwright and cricketer*) 91
Read, Norman (*walker*) 14
Reader, John (*darts player*) 148
Reardon, Ray (*snooker player*) 23, 155, 189, 191, 208, 210
Redgrave, Vanessa (*actress*) 30
Redman, Norman (*soccer referee*) 79
Red Rum (*racehorse*) 18, 73, 121, 161
Reed, Oliver (*actor*) 2, 44
Rees, Dai (*golfer*) 19
Remingo, Lindy (*athlete*) 52
Rennert, Peter (*tennis player*) 112
Revie, Don (*football manager*) 54, 140, 194
Richard, Cliff (*singer*) 16
Richards, Sir Gordon (*jockey*) 43, 105
Richards, Renee (*née Richard Raskind*) (*tennis player*) 17
Richards, Robert E. (*athlete*) 167
Richards, Viv (*cricketer*) 32
Richmond, Bill (*all-rounder*) 161
Richmond, Peter (*rugger referee*) 137
Rickaby, Fred (*jockey*) 152
Rickaby, Iris (*jockey*) 152
Riegles, Roy (*American Footballer*) 145
Riggs, Bobby (*tennis player*) 45
Roberto (*racehorse*) 152
Roberts, Kenny (*motorcyclist*) 53, 217
Robertson, Jimmy (*caddy*) 164
Robinson, John (*fat fan*) 75
Robson, Bobby (*football manager*) 9
Romark (*hypnotist*) 95, 96
Roe, Erica (*streaker*) 130, 180
Rook, Jean (*journalist*) 146
Roosevelt, Alice 35
Roosevelt, President Theodore 171
Rose, Dick (*footballer*) 86
Rosewall, Ken (*tennis player*) 203
Ross, Bill (*wrestler*) 187

# INDEX

Rothstein, Arnold (*gambler*) 36
Rubell, Steve (*discotheque owner*) 12
Russell, Joanne (*tennis player*) 14
Russie, Bernard (*skier*) 45
Ruth, Babe (*baseball player*) 58, 119, 126, 196, 197

Sabedon, Kolo (*boxer*) 77
Sadri, John (*tennis player*) 105, 106
Saharias, Babe (*golfer*) 205
Sailer, Tony (*skiing coach*) 5
Sample, Johnny (*American Footballer*) 199
Sands, Dave (*boxer*) 7
Sangster, Robert (*racehorse owner*) 142
Saunders, Dick (*jockey*) 138
Scanlon, Albert (*footballer*) 128
Scanlon, Bill (*tennis player*) 104
Schaffer, Karl (*skater*) 86
Scott, David Morgan (*football president*) 137
Scott, George C. (*actor*) 29
Scudamore, Peter (*jockey*) 52
Segrave, Sir Henry (*water speed record-holder*) 113
Seki, Kisaburo (*judo trainer*) 191
Selassie, Emperor Haile 184
Senegakali, (*rugger player*) 1
Sexton, Dave (*football manager*) 98
Shankly, Bill (*football manager*) 104, 185
Shanks, Don (*footballer*) 112
Shaw, Alfred (*cricketer*) 113
Shaw, Robert (*actor*) 29
Sheene, Barry (*motorcyclist*) 41, 53, 77, 111, 128, 153, 165, 174, 176
Sheene, Mrs Iris (*mother of Barry*) 128
Shepard, Captain Alan (*astronaut and golfer*) 186
Shepel, Anatoly (*footballer*) 125
Sheppard, Rt. Rev. David (*cricketer and Bishop*) 161, 163, 167
Shilton, Peter (*footballer*) 31, 158, 178, 189
Shoemaker, Willie (*jockey*) 93, 151
Shoemark, Bill (*jockey*) 30
Shorter, Frank (*athlete*) 34
Shranz, Karl (*skier*) 8
Shrewsbury, Arthur (*cricketer*) 113
Shwarzenegger, Arnold (*bodybuilder*) 103, 128
Sibson, Tony (*boxer*) 43, 211
Siegal, Linda (*tennis player*) 67
Simmonds, Bernie (*boxer*) 17
Simpson, Tom (*cyclist*) 19, 66
Simpson, Warren (*snooker player*) 55
Sir Ivor (*racehorse*) 151
Sitwell, Sir Osbert (*writer*) 167
Slack, Jack (*boxer*) 94
Sloniecka, Stefanja (*girlfriend of G. Best*) 20, 87
Small, Edward (*film producer*) 50
Small, Gladstone (*cricketer*) 78
Smirnov, Vladimir (*fencer*) 55
Smith, Dean (*athlete*) 52
Smith, Harvey (*showjumper*) 26, 43, 104, 171, 186
Smith, John (*American Football player*) 81

Smith, Jonathan (*boxer*) 93
Smith, Robyn (*jockey*) 84
Smith, Stan (*tennis player*) 203
Snagge, John (*commentator*) 24
Snead, Sam (*golfer*) 157
Snow, John (*cricketer*) 13, 76, 135, 154
Sobers, Sir Gary (*cricketer*) 94, 169
Solomon, Joe (*cricketer*) 52
Spencer, John (*snooker player*) 21
Spescha, Placidus E. (*mountaineer*) 167
Spinks, Leon (*boxer*) 57
Spitz, Mark (*swimmer*) 10, 44, 54, 93, 122, 127, 162, 210
Spitz, Suzy (*wife of Mark*) 210
Spock, Dr Benjamin (*child psychologist and rower*) 91
Springfield, Dusty (*singer*) 86
Spyridon, Louis (*athlete*) 161
Stackpole, Keith (*cricketer*) 175
Stadler, Craig (*golfer*) 49
Stanhope, Stephen (*jockey*) 121
Stavin, Mary (*girlfriend of G. Best*) 20, 123
Steele, David (*cricketer*) 19
Stenger, Casey (*baseball manager*) 99
Stephens, Helen (*athlete*) 15
Stephenson, Jan (*golfer*) 16
Stepney, Alex (*footballer*) 175
Sterry, Rex (*tennis official*) 119
Stewart, Jackie (*racing driver*) 19, 82
Stiles, Nobby (*footballer*) 165, 214
Stones, Dwight (*athlete*) 8
Storey, Peter (*footballer*) 212
Stove, Betty (*tennis player*) 181, 204
St Paddy (*racehorse*) 151
St Leger, Colonel Anthony 132, 133
Street, Adrian (*wrestler*) 40, 73, 187, 209
Strong, Rex (*boxer*) 95
Strong, Shirley (*athlete*) 176
Suarez, Senor (*false accuser*) 71
Sudhaus, Norbert (*bogus athlete*) 34
Summerbee, Mike (*footballer*) 30
Summerskill, Baroness (*busybody*) 141
Summonite, Stephanie (*stable girl*) 121
Surtees, John (*racing driver*) 19
Sutherland, Bob (*bowls player*) 7
Squires, Norm (*snooker player*) 12

Tanner, Roscoe (*tennis player*) 27, 114, 203
Tapscott, R.D. (*tennis player*) 79
Tavaré, Chris (*cricketer*) 44
Taylor, Bob (*cricketer*) 176
Taylor, Peter (*football trainer*) 37, 43, 124, 163, 192, 193
Taylor, Roger (*tennis player*) 114
Teenoso (*racehorse*) 152
Terry, Mrs Barbara (*hunger striker*) 173
Thatcher, Mark (*racing driver and son of Margaret*) 187

# FLYNLOCK BONES

# THE EYE OF MOGDROD

*To Sarah-Jane & Rebekah,*
*from Dad*
D.K.

*For Leesa*
M.E.

First published in Great Britain in 2021 by Scallywag Press Ltd,
10 Sutherland Row, London SW1V 4JT
Text copyright © 2021 by Derek Keilty
Illustration © 2021 by Mark Elvins
The rights of Derek Keilty and Mark Elvins to be identified
as the author and illustrator of this work have been asserted by them
in accordance with the Copyright, Designs and Patents Act, 1988
All rights reserved
Edited by Deborah Chancellor
Printed and bound in Great Britain by Clays Ltd, Elcograf S.p.A.
Printed on FSC paper
001
British Library Cataloguing in Publication Data available
ISBN 978-1-912650-67-5